Praise for *How to Build Your O*

CU00750337

"From Huxley's *Brave New Worl*
industrial Teesside has often acte
ary creative dreams. Now, in this vital and necessary cultural
history, Steve Spithray shines the light on a quixotic new
addition to the North East's industrial story - the heroic venture
in 21st-century record-making that is Middlesbrough's Press
On Vinyl. In sharp, lyrical prose, Spithray goes beyond the
weary clichés of modern music writing to celebrate a group of
people truly making it new – and pointing to a way out of their
hometown's rumoured decline in the process. This is a truly
remarkable and essential book: if Rishi Sunak and Keir Starmer
don't read it and take note of its example, we're all doomed."
Alex Niven, author and journalist

"Testament to the great ambition and passion of music lovers who
knew they could make a big and positive impact on UK music."
Chris Hawkins, BBC Radio 6 DJ

"*How To Build Your Own Record Pressing Plant* is a
compelling tale of an indie pipe dream turned reality and
a superb example of what can happen when passionate
people follow their gut. Combining local music history with a
carefully researched insight into how the often nefarious
music industry works, with plenty of nitty gritty detail for vinyl
geeks, Steve Spithray's book is at once a warts and all expose
of the early days of a business founded on a pub conversation
gone haywire, and an inspirational exploration of how a
beleaguered industry can be changed for the better."
Claire Dupree, editor of NARC Magazine

"A total inspiration. A do-it-yourself guide for builders of dreams
everywhere, full of drive, righteousness, and all the warmth of vinyl."
Richard Milward, author

"Would have made a great reality TV show."
John Esplen, Overground Records

Also by Steve Spithray

From Shrug to the Moon: the Robert Nichols Story

HOW TO BUILD YOUR OWN RECORD PRESSING PLANT

The True Story of Press On Vinyl

by Steve Spithray

First published in Great Britain in 2023
by Butterfly Effect Publishing, Darlington, England

British Library Cataloguing in Publication Data. A catalogue record for this book is
available from the British Library.

ISBN 978-1-7391004-0-7

Cover design by Rob Irish
Page design by Françoise Harvey
All photographs by Kerry Todd
Video content by Kerry Todd and Dominic Dunn

Printed by Sixth Element, Stockton-on-Tees, England

"Listen, mate, life has surface noise."
John Peel

Preface

When I bumped into a slightly worse-for-wear Henry Carden (manager of Cattle & Cane, Mt Misery and newcomers Komparrison) at a midweek gig in Middlesbrough in September 2021, my previous book about a legendary local punk singer wasn't even back from the printer. We swapped pleasantries and got chatting about the local music scene and what had been going on in the few months since we'd last seen each other, including Press On Vinyl, which I had already seen mentioned rather vaguely online.

That was when Henry pointed out Danny Lowe across the room and suggested I have a chat with him to see what we might be able to do for each other. A promise I had made to myself not to take on any bigger writing projects at least until the new year meant on this occasion I left Danny be.

However (and at this point it wasn't even an idea, more just an itch that needed scratching, or something on the tip of my tongue) what Henry had said opened a creative door in my mind. My book launch came and went in early December and then, suddenly, I had a lot of time on my hands. A couple of emails later and I found myself pitching an idea to three people I'd never met before, just before Christmas, inside the galvanics laboratory of a vinyl record pressing plant that was yet to press a single record.

Thus began my monthly visits to Press On Vinyl, compiling a thorough record of the company's first year in business, seeing things first-hand as the business grew, and speaking to Danny and the other staff.

At this stage we already had some interesting ideas floating around about marketing and design, but I was not even sure if the project would be a book or a high-end brochure. However, I did have an idea that whatever the finished product was,it would be published by a record label in order to reach the music industry audience it was always intended for.

With Henry already in my mind, I contacted Tees Music Alliance with an idea that their previously dormant TLR label might release whatever this thing was. While they were keen on the idea, they were unsure of the logistics of a literature project – but they did suggest speaking to Stephen Gill at Darlington-based Butterfly Effect Records and Scott Lewis at Leeds' Clue Records. Stephen is a philanthropic vinyl and music fanatic, who held a similar belief that there was no reason a book about the music industry should not be released by a record label. We were definitely now working on a book.

To facilitate this, he suggested bringing in Françoise Harvey, a freelance production editor and writer, to help with the production of the book.

With everything fully costed, and some favourable quotes from a couple of UK printers happy to meet our design requirements, I met with Scott at a local metropolitan multi-venue all-dayer and, three pints in, we thrashed out some ideas.

It was Scott who suggested I read David Byrne's *How Music Works*, which became something of an inspirational bible and metaphorical comfort blanket during the rest of the writing process whenever I needed to visualise how a book about Press On Vinyl could work in terms of content, design and quality. David's book is a thorough yet readable journey around all corners of the music industry that appeals to aficionados and laymen alike which is how I hope this book is also received, simultaneously aimed at music industry bods, vinyl fanatics and music lovers from all walks of life. While the Clue Records connection wasn't quite right on this occasion, Scott's early input was invaluable.

I then began editing down some 20-odd hours of audio into something more book-shaped...

Steve Spithray, December 2022

I love the Boro me,
I'm a Boro immigrant,
Spent my youth in Thornaby…

A town whose name's called after
Their Viking history,
Like this town's history,
And those along the Tees,
We've just each other's inputs, values and capabilities…

I love the Boro me,
Coz this town loves with ease.
If you're sound mate, then so am I,
And you do as you please…

Moses Carpenter made his way as a member of the Mohawk tribe,
As a member of the werld he wandered,
Skarunyate is still alive,
Coz this town is alive,
And I'm a Boro citizen, an immigrant am I,
In a world in which we thrive is tied by bonds and goings on, from
        within the town of mine, and yours, and everyone's of course,
Coz that's how it's been since day dot…

Coz I'm a Boro citizen, means my heart is warm,
As I live among these people, places and faces they have worn…

Coz I'm a Boro citizen, I love the Boro me,
Coz I'm a Boro citizen, proud immigrant is me…

Danny Lowe, 2019

CONTENTS

Prologue
Christmas Eve 2021
(Day 76)

The winter sun rises over fresh tarmac. The first light bounces off the box-fresh white lines of the empty car park and onto the striking rainbow design of Press On Vinyl's immaculate Middlesbrough HQ at the Tees Advanced Manufacturing Park (TeesAMP). It's 7am on Christmas Eve as public face and inspirational talisman of Press On Vinyl, Danny Lowe, pulls his slightly care-worn VW into his usual bay. He is already in typically effervescent mood.

And why shouldn't he be? Danny is one of the most enthusiastic music fans you could ever meet and today is a big day for him and the Press On Vinyl team: nine long months after getting the keys to the brand-new company's bespoke pressing plant, the first two pressing machines – arguably the most important piece of the mechanical jigsaw – are due to arrive, and once installed they will finally be ready to press their first record.

The new plant is spitting distance from the iconic ICI Tower, known to anyone who has ever crossed the nearby A19 flyover, and in the shadow not of the town's famous Transporter Bridge, but the equally popular vertical-lift Newport Bridge. The Newport Bridge is an industrial relic that served to allow boats to continue along the river to the old port of Stockton long after the formation of Middlesbrough as a town at the start of the steel boom, but which now serves as a local road link between the twin towns.

As recently as 1820 Middlesbrough was little more than a farm and hamlet with around 25 residents, but in 1829 a group of Quaker businessmen, crucially including Stockton and Darlington Railway shareholder Joseph Pease, bought the farmstead and established Port Darlington and the railway station. The town of Middlesbrough was born.

In 1841, Henry Bolckow and John Vaughan established the first iron foundry, and the steel boom began at pace. In 1962, William Gladstone spoke the immortal words, "this remarkable place, the youngest child of England's enterprise, is an infant, but if an infant, an infant Hercules". By the 1870s, it was producing one-third of the UK's pig iron, and the town was known as Ironopolis. The rest is, for want of a better word, history.

By the 1980s the town was at the arrowhead of northern industrial decline. In 1986 the town's football club nearly became extinct, and in 1987, Margaret Thatcher famously walked through the wilderness in nearby Thornaby, Since then the old town, now known as St Hildas, has fallen into ruin, with only the original town hall and Transporter Bridge still standing proud. More recently, since the 2019 election, the old political red wall has turned blue, putting the town at the frontline of the country's new political order as negative article after negative article in the national press use the area either as case study or an easy poverty reference.

In recent years attempts have been made to regenerate the area, with mixed success. Middlesbrough College and the Boho Zone have provided it with some quirky architecture, but developments have been mired in controversy and areas of wasteland still perforate the terrain.

The Press On Vinyl site itself is on the arterial edge of the old town, now permanently divided from the present town centre by the railway line and colloquially known as 'over the border' (or the wrong side of the tracks to everyone else).

Danny Lowe is a mainstay of the Teesside music scene, having previously played in bands, run a record label and put on gigs in the area. He can still regularly be seen holding court with bands and fans alike at local shows.

In fact, all the Press On Vinyl staff are vinyl and/or music fans, and many are also long-term associates of the management team. It was at a gig at Middlesbrough's DIY Base Camp Boro[1] venue that I became fully aware of how integral Press On Vinyl's very ethos would be in the way the business operates.

---

1   In November 2022, Base Camp Boro announced it was suspending its operations. A flood in the basement of the sprawling venue a few weeks before, along with spiralling energy bills and uncertainty over the future ownership of the building, had seemingly brought things to a head. After battling hard to survive all the COVID lockdowns, it seemed a cost-of-living crisis as well was just too much.

Ethos is a word we will see mentioned a lot in connection with the company, and theirs is something they have never been backward in coming forward about – even once (perhaps rashly) hoisting a Cuban flag on the side of the building in response to some negative press that we will hear more about later. But for now, if there is one thing Danny wants, it's that he wants you to know about Press On Vinyl.

The vinyl revival, or vinyl crisis depending which side of the coin you bet on, is not a new thing, but it has been getting progressively more troublesome for the last 25 years.

As early as 1994, when Oasis released their critically acclaimed debut album *Definitely Maybe*, an already industry-savvy Noel Gallagher released an odd number of tracks on the CD. He knew this meant the album would be a track short for a double vinyl version, and a bonus track would ensure the completists would have to buy the vinyl as well.

Fast forward to 2021 and Adele reputedly ordering 300,000 vinyl copies of her album *30* would be the straw that broke the camel's back, at least in the media. But even by 2010, independent and unsigned bands were complaining that their 100-1,000 limited pressings were being bumped down the schedules as everyone from Fleetwood Mac to Taylor Swift clogged up the European pressing plants' production lines. And they didn't have a local vinyl producer to turn to.

Vinyl initially revolutionised the recorded music industry in 1931 when RCA Victor released the first commercially available long-playing disc on 30cm flexible plastic to be played at 33.3rpm. The modern vinyl record was born. The groove technology used by vinyl records had been in place since the wax cylinders of the 1890s and was used for the 78rpm discs popularised in the 1920s. Prior to these developments, recorded music had only been available on even more unwieldy and very brittle shellac and, before that, giant cylinders of zinc and glass.

All that was really happening was that the grooves were getting smaller. And, indeed, today's upmarket record decks still use the same needle and groove methodology as the old phonograph machines, working in the same way, changing sound vibrations into electronic signals that are then amplified through speakers.

In 1948, Columbia Records began marketing the first LPs – capitalising on early demand for the songs popularised and passed around verbally between soldiers of different nationalities in the Second World War. The subsequent commercial rivalry between RCA Victor and Columbia Records led to RCA's introduction of what it intended to be a competing vinyl format: the 7" 45rpm disc.

From 1948 to 1950, in what was known as the War of the Speeds, record companies and consumers faced uncertainty over which of these formats would ultimately prevail. The 33.3rpm LP eventually became the predominant format for albums, and the 7" 45rpm disc, or 'single', established a significant niche for shorter duration discs. By the early rock 'n' roll boom of the mid-1950s, vinyl sales had already reached unexpected highs – even before single groove stereo sound was introduced in 1958, with each side of the groove providing left and right channels. The groove itself is V-shaped, with each wall carrying one of the two stereo signals. The right channel is carried by the side closest to the outside of the record while the left channel is carried by the inside wall. Literally the left and right you hear in your headphones.

Vinyl sales peaked in the mid-1970s. After that, competition from cassettes and then CDs saw vinyl sales steadily dwindle, especially from the mid-1980s when a canny marketing strategy involving Sony, Philips and Dire Straits suddenly made CDs more accessible and affordable to all. This was long before the format-less format that is MP3 made music much more available for free.

Ironically, it was the availability of MP3s that started what would become an inexorable pushback in the early 2000s, from those who wanted a physical product that complemented the fashion for retro chic. By then vinyl records could be cheaply purchased from plants in the former Eastern bloc. It was the go-to format for unsigned artists and those wanting small runs of official physical releases alongside their CD-Rs[2]. Around the same time, younger people started to inherit vinyl collections of varying sizes from family members. Vinyl records suddenly became not only a collectible commodity, but an underground cult.

Meanwhile, the record labels had realised that the holy grail of formats (the format-less format) was not the license to print money they always envisioned and soon realised that physical formats were growing in popularity: vinyl sales started to notably pick up again around 2012 as CD-Rs fell

---

2 Recordable CD technology had been available since the late 1980s, but it was the inclusion of CD recorders on laptops as standard in the early 2000s that suddenly allowed many people to start writing, or 'ripping,' their own CDs at home. On one occasion around this time, I even saw a well-known local band writing their own CD-Rs before they went on stage, to sell to fans after their set.

out of favour with small artists, and vinyl had become the cheapest way for those on a budget to get that all-important physical product out. The rest is well documented. Fleetwood Mac were one of the first big names to cash in, with multiple re-issue versions of their all-time vinyl classic *Rumours* creating an expensive headache for completists. From there you can then trace a pretty straight path to why Taylor Swift and Adele are hijacking Record Store Day. A similar cassette revival has never really taken hold.

R eaders of fiction may have read Tom Wolfe's 1987 book *The Bonfire of the Vanities*. It's a literary drama about ambition, social class, politics and greed, set in New York, and now often used as a metaphor for capitalism versus socialism. Or the big man against the little. Taken literally at the time of its publication (and at the height of the CD revolution in music) it received rave reviews for its ambitious scope and contemporary spin on a historic trope.

What it does highlight is society's almost involuntary pushback against anything that threatens the status quo, and something Press On Vinyl would become accustomed to over the following months, with its commitment to being the best regardless of industry norms and traditions. While not quite the revolutionary capitalist versus socialist story arc, Press On Vinyl's commitment to ethical business practices and job creation is borne from a paradoxical and perhaps subconscious urge to succeed, and for the greater good.

While the broader intention of Press On Vinyl is to learn and share, this approach is something that is not always agreeable to the music industry as establishment. Earlier in December, a *New Statesman* article remarked on an interaction between Danny and an industry broker who dubbed the Press On Vinyl project "the communist pressing plant of Teesside" because Danny wouldn't reduce their prices for a major label act. This is what culminated in the Cuban flag briefly being draped over the scaffolding outside the plant.

Press On Vinyl is not just a pressing plant plugging a gap in the supply side problems of the format. It is built on an ethos that sets it apart entirely from existing plants elsewhere in the world, and also from traditional relationships with the big record labels.

Firstly, it is committed to retaining a set percentage of capacity for independent acts. This is unprecedented in a satellite-industry used to depending on the major label millions.

In fact, the plant's first press will be Teesside quintet Komparrison's *You Say She's Satisfied* EP, released on 11 March 2022 (remarkably only two weeks after the originally planned release date of 28 February, and an early indicator of what a tight ship Press On Vinyl are already commanding at this stage). It's important to the team, and as a symbolic yardstick, that the first discs off the press are for a local act. Komparrison have worked tirelessly throughout the North East music scene over the past few years, going from a duo to a five-piece and becoming a mainstay on the regional festival circuit. Thus ensuring this release really is as important to them as Press On Vinyl.

A customs spot check has already meant a possible delay of delivery until 27 December which, though frustrating, would have little long-term impact: everything has already been meticulously planned to navigate bumps in the road and soothe any teething problems.

In addition, further problems caused by the shipping process mean the company has even considered having future presses delivered separately in parts, as the first two machines ended up being completely stripped and re-assembled anyway.

The pressing machines do in fact arrive on Christmas Eve, to the relief and delight of all involved (despite a last-minute Xmas party having to be shelved as "the presents arrived early for once"). It's a nice little metaphorical stocking filler in advance of the sleigh of delights Press On Vinyl already know they have in store over the coming months.

However, six weeks at sea in all temperatures has seen some water damage to the machines: protective paper separators have glued themselves onto some plastic panels and some of the rubber tubing inside the machines have snapped due to extreme temperature changes. The paper separators have to be painstakingly removed bit by bit, like peeling labels off giant plastic jam jars, and all the individual tubes and pipes checked and replaced.

For reference it can perhaps be noted that around this time another pressing plant is also preparing to open, under strict secrecy, near London. This is largely because one of the big major labels (that's one from Universal, Sony and Warner) has already block-booked capacity for one, three or five years, depending on who you listened to at the time; the complete antithesis of Press On Vinyl.

If ever a project was destined from the start for either unprecedented success or abject failure, it is Press On Vinyl. But that is to deny the intricate relationships and web of characters, wherewithal, nous and bravado that will start to quickly cement the company into local lore long before the records even begin pressing.

Danny has already talked passionately to friends about his vision for Middlesbrough. It's based loosely on the Detroit scene of the 1960s he so loves, where acts recorded their music straight to lathe and performed it live in the city, and while it seemed fantastically overstated, who's to say what might happen in the months to come?

This is Press On Vinyl's story from its inception, of how two ordinary guys went from running a tiny DIY digital label to rubbing shoulders with some of their heroes and the biggest names in the global music industry...

Day 1
9 October 2021

UK history will remember September 2021 as the month the government's job furlough scheme officially ended and the country formally returned to normal after three lockdowns of varying degrees following the COVID-19 outbreak in March 2020. For Press On Vinyl, it was the point the fledgling business became a full-time endeavour and started operating like the business we see today (albeit on a more threadbare level, with less staff, machinery and banter). It was around this time Danny Lowe finally took the plunge, put himself on the books, and quit his old life and job...

However, let's go back a bit before we go forward.

For all intents and purposes, the Press On Vinyl project is the brainchild of Danny and fellow Managing Director, David Todd (Toddy), who received the keys to the cavernous warehouse way back in March 2021.

Wait, first, let's go even further back, to a discussion over a couple of pints between the two directors that first sowed the seeds of this extraordinary venture.

To understand how the grass grows you need to study its roots. Danny and Toddy had been running a digital record label on Teesside called Goosed when, in late 2019, they decided to release their first physical product: a vinyl compilation album featuring all their acts to date.

There is something so totally and purely grassroots about compilation albums that it seemed like a no-brainer – until they discovered that the waiting times at the record pressing plants meant the vinyl would not be available for a pre-Christmas release. Not only that, but the way the bumping system worked for small vinyl runs at geographically distant pressing plants also meant the plants couldn't guarantee 100% that the records would be back in time for *next* Christmas.

Danny and Toddy cursed the fact there was no way of just pressing a small batch locally. It was at that precise moment the first grass seed was sown: what if *they* could do that?

At first Toddy considered buying a small portable press to produce extremely limited runs locally, but over the following months the idea just wouldn't go away. The pair researched more and more details, with Toddy in particular spending many hours each week trouble shooting, workshopping and networking potential business plans and operational models. By now David Hynes (another Press On Vinyl director, early backer, and Danny's former boss) was already working on financial profiles and business projections with a view to investing.

"I only did it because Danny told me to," Toddy said to me, only half-joking – an early insight into the pair's relationship, which is really the foundation of Press On Vinyl.

Skipping forward to October 2021, the building has an air of Willy Wonka's chocolate factory. Inside the floor is painted Transporter Blue (in-house designer Tommy McMillan scraped a flake of paint off the town's iconic Transporter Bridge and had the exact colour reproduced) and everything felt and smelt very new. There is a galvanics lab in the middle of the huge warehouse that will initially be lined by four pressing machines running off up to 1,000 records each per day overseen, for now, by renowned Italian pressing expert Franco Sironi.

The metal stampers the galvanics lab will produce are not an exact science, but Franco has over 40 years in the business (many with EMI during the vinyl heyday of the 1980s). At 67 years old, he has a vision to make Press On Vinyl the best pressing plant in the world before he retires in three years time.

Franco founded his company, Media Commodities & Services (MCS) SRL[3], in Milan in 1999. At present it is the only company in the world able to supply the entire chain of machinery for vinyl production, due in part to its relationship with M-Tech Engineering in Hong Kong. Both companies are essential to Press On Vinyl's operations.

---

3   MCS is focused on introducing and developing new products for the media industry, whilst continuing to supply used equipment for the optical disc industry. In 2020, the company started working on a new line of products dedicated to vinyl production. The machines created by MCS are purposefully simple and modern and designed for start-up companies, so it's little surprise Franco was keen to work with Press On Vinyl to showcase his products.

Around the same time they put themselves on the books as salaried directors, Danny and Toddy had danced the night away with a who's who of Teesside scenesters at a gig at Base Camp Boro (just around the corner, in Middlesbrough's up-and-coming Exchange Square), before ending up back at the Press On offices for an impromptu after-party and kickabout with headliners Opus Kink.

These work-hard/play-hard shenanigans (including the very premature 60-day countdown that started in April, with people doing online videos of themselves doing daft stuff like the crab while namedropping the company, or pop-up barbershops in the office space) blighted the company's early social media campaigns, but some funding and support from Colin Oliver's Futuresound Group, a music management and promotions company based in Leeds, as well as a more savvy (and expensive) PR campaign via Harry Ridgway's Hanglands PR, had by now at least seen much of the daftness put on the back burner – even if, when I asked Tommy what he was most looking forward to over the next year, he answered, "all the parties we get invited to". In my early visits to the plant, Tommy would become an almost reassuringly constant presence as a kind of mellow hype man, as Danny was invariably called away to fix one small problem or another.

Tommy, to give him the credit he deserves also talked passionately and candidly about how he was excited just to live the dream and work with some equally passionate people he has known for years – a branch of the general Press On Vinyl ethos of inclusivity. For example, Tommy and Danny had known engineer Kilvo (Andy Kilvington, Operations Engineering Manager) since school, and Danny cherrypicked him from a job on Morrison's delivery wagons for the role...

I spoke to Harry Ridgway a couple of months later, and he was very enthusiastic about the opportunity to work with Press On Vinyl.

"Futuresound is how we ended up being involved," he says. "We had already been involved in some cool stuff in Boro with [band] Nel Unlit and [indie record publisher] Spooker Rekkids releases. We didn't know the Press On guys prior to our involvement. but Colin called me up, explained the project and asked if we could help manage the messaging and put one press release out [the famous mission statement in May 2021] that happily turned into us working very closely with everyone for over six months."

From my first visit, long before the arrival of the pressing machines, Danny, Tommy and videographer Kerry Todd stayed back after hours to accommodate my work commitments, excitedly showing me around the sprawling network of office and factory spaces that over the coming months would become their home from home. We congregated in the unfinished galvanics lab as I nervously explained how I wanted to record their first year in business if not for posterity but for Teesside. They, in turn, eagerly told me their plans, which were clearly already firmly in place.

With Futuresound's investment topping up a total initial investment in excess of £1.5m (including the purchase of up to five pressing machines and a new live-to-lathe aspect, which they hoped would be completed by August 2022) it was clear that at this stage Press On Vinyl was heavily reliant on third-party support. Futuresound came with an impressive music industry CV[4], with not only years of experience in the live music sector, but also in ticketing, artist management and a record label. It certainly seemed like a match made if not in heaven, then somewhere close to the music industry's promised land.

Danny and Toddy had done a couple of pitch events on Zoom during the pandemic. In the first one, Danny did the talking while Toddy answered the questions (being too nervous to do the presentation). Before the second event, Toddy had been at work all night. He nearly turned Zoom off, and was going to tell Danny they'd had no luck. However, he made himself do it and it just so happened Colin Oliver from Futuresound was there. Colin later said the same – that he was listening to a lot of boring pitches, and only stayed on the call out of a curious interest in Toddy's pitch. He finally invested on the day that another loan offer, only open for three months and dependent on additional funding being confirmed, was due to expire.

Around the same time as the Futuresound investment was realised in May, along with the deal with Leeds-based

---

4 Futuresound is Yorkshire's largest live music brand, which has been hosting concerts across Leeds and Yorkshire for over 20 years. The company regularly puts on over 400 shows a year, and has worked with a number of world-famous acts, from its first gig in the region, to arena and large-scale outdoor shows. Futuresound-run events include Live at Leeds Festival, Live at The Piece Hall in Halifax, The Leeds United Centenary Celebration at Elland Road Stadium, and the biggest headline shows in Leeds in 13 years, when Ed Sheeran played two nights at Roundhay Park in 2019. At time of writing, the company were promoting Newcastle's Rock and Roll Circus series, including shows by Noel Gallagher and The Libertines. The company's other brands include Slam Dunk and its associated festival, as well as Somewhere Presents.

Hanglands PR, a more professional approach from Press On Vinyl started to take shape. This was particularly on Press On's Instagram and Facebook accounts where informative and educational videograms became the norm amongst more playful playlist and 'meet the team' features.

At the end of May, the mission statement[5] that outlined the new company's raison d'être and dual passions for music and Middlesbrough was released, and had some local commentators speculating that Resolution Media, the usual PR suspects Teesside-ways, had been brought in to steer the publicity ship. However, little did anyone know at that stage what had actually been happening in the background. It was not until 15 September 2021 that the Futuresound partnership was announced.

The new, more nuanced, approach to the company's socials began by sharing a handful of news articles (including one from *New Statesman* on 17 September about the state of the

---

5   The full mission statement reads: "There are 2 passions at the centre of everything we do at Press On Vinyl... MUSIC and MIDDLESBROUGH. This passion drives our mission to provide the best sounding vinyl products on the market from a regional base. For many years Middlesbrough's heritage was very much industrial and centred around pioneering engineering innovation, and we are delighted to be bringing highly skilled, precision manufacturing back to Teesside. At Press On Vinyl we have invested heavily in the latest cutting edge vinyl production machinery and software, whilst also utilising the best tried and tested methods in order to achieve this aim. Everyone in the Press On Vinyl Family also has a passion and drive to provide the highest level of customer service built on equality and transparency. There are well documented problems with the vinyl supply chain, and aside from increasing capacity for production we are committed to providing high quality vinyl for artists and labels big and small. We are here to see Middlesbrough and the Music Industry Press On."

vinyl industry that would be a sign of things to come, followed by a Toddy interview in the *iPaper* on 27 September, which outlined the 100-3,000 run sizes for the first time). By the end of September, the company's distinct signage had been installed on the outside front corner of the building where the office entrance is, designed by Tommy and manufactured by Fox Creative[6]. Kerry's atmospheric drone footage of the outside of the plant then really started to provide a feel for how the plant would be received, its distinctive colours visible from up to a mile away in all directions…

So although they'd received the keys to the Press On building in March, following the brand-denting 60-day countdown it was not until October that things started to look a bit more formulated and business-like, with Press On Vinyl sponsoring the Westgarth 1[7] stage at Middlesbrough's multi-venue all-day music festival Twisterella.

At this point, a handful of in-the-know folk who had visited the plant were drip-feeding positivity about the project, and the local grapevine started to do its work. It would be a relatively inconspicuous start for Press On Vinyl, with the Westgarth Stage most notable that day for local acts Jodie Nicholson and Mt Misery's gentle indie being drowned out by an over-zealous early crowd (although fair play to the stage invader during Jodie's set, who gave the

---

6   Fox Creative have over 20 years' experience within the sign, print and advertising industry, specialising in distinctive designs and corporate branding.

7   Middlesbrough's famous Westgarth Social Club closed its doors for the last time in February 2023. In recent years the two-roomed venue had boasted the likes of Catfish & The Bottlemen, The Vaccines, First Aid Kit and Wolf Alice passing through on early national tours. It first opened in 1911.

audience a sweary telling off for talking over her set. She would be welcome at Press On Vinyl any time, no doubt). For reference, the headliner on the Westgarth stage that day was alt-rock band Fatherson.

On 12 October, *Press On Vinyl TV*: Episode 1 appeared on YouTube. This was a two-and-a-half-minute time-lapse video of the galvanics lab being built in the middle of the large empty warehouse, while the iconic Transporter Blue paint is mixed and applied to the large floorspace.

Then, on 26 October, a few choice Toddy quotes in a longform *Mixmag*[8] article about the difficulty of getting vinyl records pressed despite the industry being at its strongest for decades, began a much more orchestrated upward media curve…

The QR codes found at the end of some chapters of this book will take you to exclusive video content from Press On Vinyl that is relevant to what you've just read.

---

8   'The Vinyl Straw: Why The Vinyl Industry Is At Breaking Point', Megan Townsend, 25 October 2021, https://mixmag.net/feature/vinyl-industry-record-breaking-point-manufacturing

Day 35
13 November 2021

As well as the distinctive exterior and Transporter Blue floor paint being applied, October and November at the Press On plant were most notable for large-scale building works in the factory. The breeze block wall that would separate the pressing operation from the complex plumbing works appeared, as did the 'Be Fair, Be Sound' banner, painted in big black letters on the distinctive yellow wall at the office-end of the factory and signposting the company's ethics and the FairSound imprint that they hoped would revolutionise online vinyl sales.

On the Press On socials – Facebook and Instagram primarily – there were also the beginnings of a hearts-and-minds operation to familiarise followers with all of the staff and not just those in the national papers. This started with the Office Stereo[9] feature, which highlighted the team as, first and foremost, music lovers. A mix of established artists and underground names, a trend that would continue as the feature gained traction and continued to highlight Press On's commitment to new music while also acknowledging the bigger music industry picture.

By now Emma (Lowe, Office Manager and Danny's wife), Gareth (Harrison, Sales Manager), Danny, Toddy, Kilvo and Tommy were full-time on site. The galvanics lab was a building work in progress after it was moved to the imposing central floor location it now occupies. Work in the originally planned location – in what is now the live room – was never started, after it was decided that that space could be better used in future if/when a lathe was installed.

The galvanics lab would essentially be a room within a room that, viewed outside of the context of the pressing plant, looked like any science laboratory you might find in a school or university. However, on closer inspection, it looked like many electroplating set-ups in large factories that produce their own metal plating in production. Any contamination from dust or any other foreign objects can be expensive to fix and also potentially hazardous, so the sealed environment is a vitally important factor in the process that, in this case, will eventually produce the vinyl records.

The galvanics build would be finished in November, with a big front window installed that allowed anyone on the factory floor to see what was going on in the sealed, dust-free lab.

---

9 The first feature included Frank Carter and The Rattlesnakes, Garbage, Deep Tan, 1000 Watts, Michael Kiwanuka, Opus Kink, Ruth Lyon, Steve Gunn and Yard Act amongst others, and remains, essentially, just a list of what has been popular on the office stereo.

Journalists and film crews were also starting to come down to the plant to do interviews as the publicity machine started to build up a head of steam. At the same time, the complex plumbing that would be essential to the pressing process was being installed by local builders and contractors organised by Uncle Nige (Nigel Yawson, Project Manager).

It was also around this time that Press On Vinyl really started coming to people's attentions locally beyond the relatively small and niche local music and vinyl scene. This was in part through a short feature with Toddy on Tyne Tees News, and an interview on the Tees Valley Business website[10] where the director talked about Futuresound's investment, while further explaining the Press On ethos to anyone caring to watch or read. Baby steps, but steps for sure.

Other people inexplicably started dropping in to visit the Press On offices unannounced – perhaps because they knew how hospitable Danny, Toddy and the team were, or perhaps just on the off-chance, to get a sneaky peek. Which is partly how charity fundraiser SpeedoMick (aka Michael Cullen) came to visit in late November, stopping off during a 2,000-mile charitable stomp around the UK and Ireland wearing only his swimming trunks. It is his Everest quote[11] that now adorns the office wall for all visitors to see.

Gareth regaled me months later with how this actually came about, and it was in typical Press On fashion. Mick was at the Transporter Bridge trying to cross the river as part of his charity walk route, but obviously without knowing that

---

10 'Spinning A New Record For Teesside's Manufacturing Industry', https://www.teesvalleybusiness.com/case-study/press-on-vinyl/
11 "I've never climbed a mountain in me life, but I know I can climb Mount Everest."

the bridge had been closed for years. As luck would have it, Kilvo, who recognised Mick from YouTube, happened to be walking past and invited him back to Press On HQ for a cuppa. I soon came to realise that Kilvo's occasionally bemused enjoyment of these kinds of random occurrences would stand him in good stead over the months that followed.

Even more extraordinarily, Mick had arranged for the BBC to come and film him that day, so he hastily rearranged for the camera crew to come over to Press On, rather than the Transporter Bridge. There, he put on a bit of a show, and garnered another fortuitous and invaluable bit of early national publicity for Press On Vinyl.

Late November also saw another Toddy interview with Chris Hawkins on BBC Radio 6 Music, while over on Facebook, the first Meet the Staff feature would further ingrain the characterful staff into our wider consciousness. This feature started with Danny, naturally, but would go on to include the entire team over the coming months. Nobody ever said socialism didn't start at the top. Well, maybe Marx…

Day 62
10 December 2021

The remainder of the year was perhaps relatively quiet compared with what was to come. Scheduled work continued apace to ready the factory floor for the delivery of the first two pressing machines, while Franco beavered away in the now complete galvanics lab, trying to perfect the mixes, timings and temperatures of the biochemical baths that would produce the all-important metal stampers that would, in turn, press the records. They were starting to cause some amount of stress as whenever one problem was seemingly fixed, another reared its head. The laborious and often soul-destroying test work in the lab was fraught with minute discrepancies and completely unpredictable variables, ranging from chemical recipes in the baths to changes in humidity in the lab, as we will see in more detail later. Some attempts showed hairline distortion, and even some holes in the finished plates. Franco returned to Italy over the new year period for a well-earned break and, in his absence, the local team managed to get an almost-perfect test plate.

With orders already starting to come in it was a relief that they still had time to troubleshoot.

In the office, the team were busy making the finishing touches to the sales process, then rethinking it and doing it again with all the changes and tweaks, until it was just right. Already nothing was being done by halves, and no stone was being left unturned in terms of finding the right way.

In his marketing role, Gareth was drumming up interest in Press On. He had in fact been on site since February 2021, and the work had soon started to build as the Press On Vinyl rumours began spreading locally by word of mouth. Local promoter and DJ Adam Gallagher was also involved at this time helping Gareth with the early PR and marketing campaigns. Although his role was short lived, especially once the nightclubs reopened after COVID, he was another important cog in an increasingly big wheel due to his myriad connections and addictive personality.

With the first two pressing machines now scheduled for December delivery, this all, conversely, gave them plenty of time to announce the Komparrison EP, which would become the first record to be pressed in Middlesbrough. The EP's release date was pencilled in for late February. If Danny and Toddy had known at this time what was round the corner in the new year, they might have savoured the small lull, but as it was, they were keeping themselves busy with the galvanics, which was one thing they were able to progress — if at little more than a snail's pace at times.

Danny told me much later that this was still an important time for them to perfect and familiarise themselves with the plant set up that would become second nature to them over the coming months, whilst also getting fully ready for everything in a mechanical capacity so they could hit the ground running as soon as the pressing machines arrived and were calibrated. That was the plan.

On 4 December, Episode 2 of *Press On Vinyl TV* featured a mesmerising video of the silvering machine (more of which later), and a week later a live music partnership was announced with local Middlesbrough venue Sticky Fingers, promising exclusives and instore performances throughout 2022.

Day 97
14 January 2022

When I returned, shortly after the New Year hangovers had dissipated, as if by serendipity – but mainly because this is what they had been doing all week – Kilvo and Man (Sheung Man Lui, the M-Tech founder who had been hired to oversee the setting up of the pressing machines – there isn't much he doesn't know about them) were out on the plant floor still stripping and replacing plastic tubes from the two pressing machines, which had arrived on Christmas Eve after all.

Kilvo (beckoning me over): "You can see there are cracks in it. They look like they've been dried up and split. It looks like it's been cut, but I think it's been frozen in the container. It was on a ship for weeks, over the Arctic route!"

I could see Man and Kilvo were already cementing a successful working relationship despite language barriers, and it was uncommon on my visits not to be greeted by either or both of them grinning about something going on in the factory that day. Nothing seemed to phase them, despite what must have been a hugely stressful time trying to set up the pressing machines and a lot to learn, for Kilvo in particular.

Tommy explained that it had been a similarly painstaking story in the galvanics lab, as they continued to iron out all the fine details. During one week in early January, Franco and the lab workers had been struggling to get the formulas in the baths right. They had still been producing stampers with occasional holes, marks and lines. Basically, they weren't producing the same results from one stamper to the next, despite there being very few environmental variables and despite following exactly the same processes in the lab. It was now 12 days since the pressing machines had arrived, although Tommy assured me, "they are getting plugged in tomorrow!"

While he wasn't directly involved in the galvanics process itself, Man's work was key to Press On being able to use the silver stamper effectively to press the hot vinyl pucks into the vinyl records we buy in the shops.

Man has a degree-level background in engineering, and in 2004 set up his M-Tech Engineering[12] company with the aim of designing and manufacturing fully and semi-automated

---

12   Man's Allegro I production line has been successfully rolled out to select customers internationally. The new Allegro II production line, which is a steam and non-steam compatible system with automated and manual operation, is compatible with 7", 10" and 12" vinyl production. The system is also designed with energy saving in mind, another aspect of their ethos that matches closely with Press On's. It is this Allegro II production line that is installed at the plant.

optical disc production equipment and CD moulds. Since 2015 the company has worked in co-operation with Franco's MCS and together they have developed the world's first fully automated steam vinyl production line, which is where the Press On Vinyl plumbing system comes into play.

M-Tech's other products include the revolutionary Glass CD, which aims to provide the listener with the ultimate song signal and almost zero loss to distortion, making the best-ever quality of the format. This is something Danny and I would also talk about, with regards to Press On Vinyl also cutting CDs on site eventually. Another indication of Press On's commitment to the maximum enjoyment of the music and product; the company will not necessarily be kettled or restricted to the vinyl format, as long as the quality of sound remains.

Danny and Toddy had also begun a similarly laborious process of interviewing for suitably qualified engineers, electro-forming specialists and plant/machinery operators from amongst hundreds of applications. They had also spent the past two weeks working out shift patterns for everyone as the company's growth projections were already starting to come to fruition.

December's *New Statesman* feature on the company had been widely read beyond dedicated vinyl fanatics, starting the new year off with a publicity bang. And the Komparrison EP had gone live for pre-orders on an early beta version of FairSound, via the band's Linktree landing page.

FairSound

At this time, FairSound was intended to be a completely separate company and website to Press On Vinyl. However, this would change back and forth a number of times over the coming months until the directors finally settled on FairSound.com. Toddy had also appeared on Kirsty Lang's BBC Radio 4 show to talk about, well, records and continue to spread the publicity butter to the far corners of the music industry toast.

FairSound didn't sound dissimilar to Myspace or Bandcamp (or Rough Trade's online presence) but in reality the side-project already potentially offered so much more than Press On itself – on a local level foremost, as an access point for local acts, but also outside of any geographic restrictions by removing the need for a middleman between vinyl production and vinyl sales, and then acting as a broker for everything else, whether that be merch or any other online campaigns...

The FairSound concept was something Danny already saw as being likely to overtake the plant as the primary business concern, keen as he always is to keep things moving forward.

In my opinion FairSound was already a brilliantly philanthropic stance for the company to take, and it would put Press On Vinyl in the zeitgeist of artist development alongside the practical advantages of being able to press the records on site. A blend of crowdfunding and social media, it was to allow acts to network, crowdfund, sell merch and generally make their products available all within the safe space of the Press On Vinyl marketplace.

Tommy had been working on FairSound that very day, trying to design a landing page before a freelance designer, Mark O'Connell, came in to put together a dummy website. Kerry and Toddy were in the far corner of the office poring over some intricate costings and the finer details of the platform.

Even at this early stage, FairSound had an advantage over its competitors by being able to offer commission-free vinyl sales to artists who had already used Press On to press their records. And being attached to the pressing plant also meant they would be able to work pressing times into the ordering system. As Danny explained in more detail:

"FairSound is going to be the digital ordering platform where bands can crowdfund campaigns [to get their records pressed], but there will also be another service on there where bands take all of the profits on the vinyl. The margins for us will be the merch and other things that they sell on that platform. Other people offer similar opportunities, but without the pressing plant attached, so those platforms are still at the back of the queue in terms of accessing the pressing plants. It will effectively give bands that aren't on a label the chance to become their own label. Eventually we'd like to make it so that when they crowdfund, the public are actually investing in the band..."

The idea of the public investing in an artist was a relatively new concept to me, and not something I'd thought about before. When I followed up on the idea a couple of months later Toddy told me that it could be done by buying into future royalties, or something similar to how Patreon works, where fans can sign up for exclusive content through a membership scheme.

It seemed very much just an idea at this stage, but something he was keen to keep on the backburner, at least when he told me about it: "The idea is for artists to be able to sell future royalty shares and streams to help fund recordings – which is what you do when you go to a record label anyway – but to do it directly with fans. We could do it through NFTs as well, so like blockchain linked to royalty shares. Then if the owners want to sell them on when the NFT is worth more they can, but the kickback always goes back to the artist. Not something we definitely *won't* be doing, but we can't do everything at once and that will take a lot of thought. It would be mint to do it eventually, though."

Further evidence of how far outside the box Danny and Toddy are always thinking, if nothing else.

Not every band on FairSound would necessarily even get a record pressed. FairSound was to be a safe and reliable middleman where people could meet each other and network but the possibilities at least in Danny's and Toddy's heads were infinite...

Danny: "Some bands will pay for their own records outright and then sell them on FairSound. We will also offer direct to fans, so bands don't have to take all the records and we can send them out for them also cutting out distro costs. We're really looking at ways we can give it away. If a band gets a record pressed that's where we make our money."

In that respect FairSound was not intended to be a money-making enterprise at all but more of a philanthropic distribution platform supported by other aspects of the business. Press On Vinyl weren't exactly giving anything away for free but having already been paid to produce the vinyl they were pledging not to then take a further commission for the records being sold through their own distribution network. Furthermore, artists would not have to pay for anything until their campaign hit what the team were calling the 'Press On Point', which was set at 65% of the campaign total.

Danny: "It's been testing this month and should be properly live by June which suits us because by then we will have four presses. FairSound will outgrow Press On if we do it right."

In the first couple of weeks of the new year, Toddy was also looking into the way people sign up to FairSound so that every user would be accountable, but without having to upload ID. Open banking provides third-party financial service providers (in this instance, FairSound) access to consumer banking, transaction and other financial data from banks and non-financial institutions (bands/artists) through Application Programming Interfaces (APIs) and is at the forefront of banking innovation. Put simply, FairSound users would verify who they were by registering with a bank account as a way of tracing accountability. So users could still go by usernames, but if anything untoward or unsavoury happened on the site it wouldn't be anonymous to the admin team.

Danny: "Safe place, man. Facebook and Twitter are reactive, not proactive. Bands can be very competitive, and it stops people setting up fake bands to attack other bands they don't like. For under-18s. they will still need bank details to sell the records so they will need their parents or whoever to verify it if they don't have an account themselves. We don't think it will deter anyone [from registering] because it is there to protect them. We know there are a lot of very young bands and artists who may not have bank accounts for other reasons, from when we had the record label. We've got a company developing it who've done this kind of thing before, and we've got an in-house guy [Mark O'Connell] who just gets everything and is passionate and very open minded to it..."

Tommy: "FairSound could be the game-changer. A way to change and shape the market and the internet in general."

Danny may laugh heartily at this wild overstatement, but they are both only half joking and Danny quickly reverts back to script: "It goes back to the same thing that none of us are doing this for money, prestige or personal gain, so it is easier doing those sort of things and the people that have invested in Press On are exactly the same as well... Franco and Man are going to sell their machines to other people as well, so the plan is to have a couple of other plants in other continents that share a similar kind of ethos that we can share our back ends with and some of the front end systems. We would give those plants the orders that come from that continent, so it could become a global thing quite easily..."

While on something of a tangent, what Danny was outlining is another important aspect of the Press On mission. The bigger picture. Press On Vinyl will never reach a point of status quo where they are producing 'x' records a day at 'y' percentage points while they all just come to work and take home a healthy pay packet at the end of the month. There will always be more or, to paraphrase the Merry Pranksters, something "furthur". This prompted me to ask Danny where he saw the business in, say, five years' time.

"The same as we are doing now just a million times different," he said. "We'll have definitely achieved a level of sustainability by then and if we haven't, we will have failed a little bit. We will have done a lot more globally with FairSound projects at other plants in other countries. The next thing we are looking at locally is taking some apprentices on so they will be time-served by then and that is something we are really passionate about."

In fact, later in the year, the first potential apprentice candidates would start coming in for training days. In terms of departmentalising, Danny seemed wary not to separate anything too soon but admitted they would soon start struggling with the pressing operation and FairSound running at such close parallels. Before the year was out, they would already be looking at how to get some extra office space to accommodate the extra freelance staff that had been brought in to help roll out FairSound beta in October 2022.

Of FairSound at this time, Danny was a man who clearly knew his onions. "What they do pay [for record pressing], everybody pays in advance, we didn't realise that until we started. Most people pay in advance now for multiple reasons, but mainly to guarantee their slot. We haven't stipulated that; it's just how the industry is working." The tense Danny used here was interesting, as it left wriggle-room for change in the future. "We had one label offer to pay their full year's quota for all their bands in advance because even the smaller labels have an obligation to their artists and if they have an artist they think will do well but don't fulfil their obligations then the band can walk away. And if they have included a vinyl run in the contract then that is another thing. We declined the offer, by the way, because we don't need to do that. That's where FairSound comes in again, and we hope that labels will start using FairSound, as well as individual artists."

In late June 2022, I asked Danny again whether there had been any movement of the upfront payment policy, particularly as the company had pledged to support local and small artists who might not always have the cash upfront. But Danny was clear that the fundamental aspect of FairSound was to crowdfund releases during the 16-week lead time, with the option of pausing the process if necessary.

While he remained open to helping those struggling on a case-by-case basis, the upfront payment policy would remain, with the FairSound set-up deemed a satisfactory workaround: "We'll have a bit of a traffic light system where we can see what money is going in and where the crowdfunders are, but once something is in the schedule it will very rarely get moved unless there is a problem with the raw products or the printing parts."

I suddenly realised how very much he was already becoming the factory boss. I felt the reality of running a business had started seeping into his subconscious as he continued: "The movement might come from having two products within a couple of weeks of each other, but they are both on red vinyl – so we would do them on the same day to save us purging the extruders and cleaning everything out. But that would be down to the efficiency of the plant as opposed to who is a more valued customer.

"We've got some very switched-on lads to manage that, and the new intake of people who have actually done things in the industry or at least *an* industry. However, if we are already doing something one way and we are having success, we are not scared to press on like that."

It was unclear if the pun was intentional, but it was another example of the ruthless independence that courses through the Press On Vinyl veins.

"All the people that are here are doers. Not just music fans, people who do. Beno [Adam Bennett, Logistics Manager] and Clancy [Paul Clance, Packing and Logistics] aren't music fans necessarily, but they're people that we know, and know how eager they are, and that is one of the main boxes ticked straight away. To say we've got a [galvanics] laboratory running at 95% in the time we have done it, with very little experience... it's a very strange one and sometimes you genuinely don't know what to do for the best, but only time will tell."

By early spring it seemed like there was a constant stream of visitors tapping at the glass office doors. Press On Vinyl's ethos of inclusivity and sharing knowledge is to be admired, but the truth is the visitors were people either in the know, or from trusted extended social networks. However, their reach and appeal were already starting to spread much further afield.

Around this time a couple of lads flew over from Brisbane in Australia to have a look. Word was, upon asking what all the plumbing gear was for[13], they had a bit of a shock how cool everything needs to be kept in the plant. Apparently, Brisbane is a little less wintry than Middlesbrough and their plans for a similar plant there might well have needed some more thought.

Musical polymath and local hero Oli Heffernan also visited. Oli has played with Mike Watt of Stooges fame as well as performing all over Europe with Ajay Saggar's King Champion Sounds, and is something of a vinyl aficionado. He had already visited a similar plant in Holland and, by all accounts, was impressed with what he saw at Press On Vinyl even at this relatively early stage.

I caught up with Oli shortly after his visit. He told me: "The attention to detail was amazing and the whole place had a really good feel about it, a bit like Willy Wonka's Chocolate Factory compared to the other pressing plants in Europe I've been to. I've since heard a couple of the records they have pressed, and they sound and look as good as any of the other records I've seen and heard, and I've seen and heard a lot of records! Plus, they are doing great things for the area and for record production in general and it will definitely help with the wait times for new releases, and [kudos] for the 'no queue

---

13   Traditionally, the moulds used to stamp records are heated by steam which is delivered to the press from a boiler at the desired 285° Fahrenheit so the moulds can melt the PVC pucks that then are pressed into a record before an aqua cooling system brings them back down to room temperature within a few seconds, to stop the discs warping. While steamless versions of the same process are new to the industry and/or still under development, Press On's commitment to sustainability has always taken into account ways to repurpose the excess steam elsewhere along with longer-term commitments to solar and waterpower. Toddy would eventually start looking at ways to use solar power to replace the steam all together.

jumping, regardless of who you are' policy which is a massive plus for me."

Stuart Willoughby of Stockton's legendary shop Sound It Out Records (itself the feature of a cult docufilm in 2011, called *Sound It Out*) also turned up one morning unannounced. Stuart is a well-known vinyl collector, vintage stereo buff and music history expert. By his own account he was equally impressed when he emailed me to say: "I was blown away by how much preparation and skill had gone into the factory preparation. I've not visited a pressing plant before, and Danny took me through each step of the fascinating process that goes into producing a vinyl record. I must admit that I'm still not exactly sure how it's done! I can imagine that the company will only get bigger. Given the exposure that Press On is getting in the press, I'm sure we'll soon have a recognised name in the industry right on our doorstep; one to rival the famous 1970s RCA plant in Washington[14]. Press On is a massive boost to the music scene in our part of the world. I hope the plant goes on to be a major player on a national – and international – level. There's also an undeniable feeling of pride seeing 'Made in Teesside' on anything. We're an industrious bunch of people.

"Press On's ethos of producing limited vinyl runs, which gives acts the opportunity to get their music out there, is an important step on the road to hopefully being

---

14   RCA's pressing plant in Washington, Tyne & Wear opened in May 1970 and was, at the time, the most modern factory of its type in the world. Computer controlled, the plant boasted twelve 12" presses and six 7" presses. In its prime the plant employed 300 staff. By the late 1970s demand for vinyl was declining, although legend has it the death of Elvis Presley in 1977 led to a reprieve from closure before the plant did finally close its doors in 1981.

discovered on a wider scale and perhaps being signed on a major label. That said, it's also just nice to have a record in your collection that's been produced by friends and made right here in our community. I wrote a bestseller a few years ago, and one of the biggest thrills I still get from the whole experience is just seeing my book on a bookshelf. I have an archive of local artists' work, and the vinyl section is woefully underrepresented. I'm hoping Press On can rectify that."

Franco was due back in the office the following day after a well-earned Christmas break with his family back in Italy. He had been treating Press On Vinyl like his own little baby and got on like a house on fire with Danny. To be fair everyone gets on like a house on fire with Danny and that's why his position within the company is so inspired. He's constantly raising the mood and keeping morale high.

By now, the company was about eight months on from those first faltering social media posts, which Danny and Toddy now openly acknowledged they didn't need to do so quickly. They were right. Although their hearts were totally in the right place, the immature skits and a 60-day countdown with no definite plan or concrete finance in place was foolhardy at best and, at worst, threatened the integrity of the fledgling business just when they needed some solid local support.

Tommy had already admitted they got the countdown way too short, starting at 60 days when it could have been any number. "But we keep saying this is the best bit where all the mistakes happen and you're working stuff out because eventually all we're going to be doing is pressing records..."

So, along with Futuresound's investment came a tidy bit of PR that would wipe the social media slate clean to pave the way for what would become, in time, a uniquely insightful foot-in to the company via its social media presence. Videographer Kerry's informative clips and genuinely interesting updates would start really laying the foundations of the social footprint and sense of community that is now so important to the Press On Vinyl brand.

While Tommy was always reliably positive, bouncing around like Tigger, Danny was equally enthusiastic about how far everything had come since December. "The galvanics stuff is now 97% there. For a chemical process it's very organic. It's like the baths have got their own lives. I know it's scientific and raises PHs and so on; densities and surface tensions are massive things – but it's almost as if they have their own will and you've got to understand them to grow and develop them. They settle in over time, and then temperature and humidity changes make a massive difference, so you've got to monitor that. It will probably be another 12-18 months before we have a full grasp of what the seasonal cycle does to it as well.

"We tweaked the temperatures yesterday and today in one of the baths to try and change the timings, because as you decrease the temperature the amp output decreases as well but you can increase the time and [get the same results], then we decreased the time but increased the temperature and [still] got the same result, so it's a lengthy process to become really efficient."

Arriving at the plant I accidentally walked into one of the interviews, thinking the interviewee was just another visitor like me. With hindsight I wondered why the interview was taking place in the main office and not a private room elsewhere. Danny told me: "We advertised for some jobs but for the first time we're looking for specific skills. Kilvo has a wealth of engineering knowledge, as does Man who builds the machines, but there is going to be too much for them on their own, so we've got three more interviewees coming in tomorrow who have similar experience with electroforming[15], not records but plating, and two others with experience of running mechanical lines, steel pressing and stuff like that. People who can work bell to bell and won't be put off by a problem.

"The plant will run 24/7 from some point in February and although we'll still be down here 12 to 16 hours a day, we still need to go and get some sleep and have some sort of life at some point."

The first person they had employed was Sales Manager Gareth, in January 2021, but his role had quickly evolved to include liaising with labels rather than direct marketing. While Gareth may joke that he has never had a sales job like it, he knows pretty much everything there is to know about the local music scene. It was also an indicator of how job titles and roles within the plant were constantly changing in line with business needs.

Out on the floor, Kilvo and Man were still inspecting the rubber tubing on the pressing machines that were damaged during transportation. Danny: "It appears there was a tank with a bit of water left in it [on the ship] and because it's

---

15   Electroforming, or electroplating, in vinyl record manufacturing is the process of using electrically charged liquid to transfer metal in a solution onto a solid. In this case, on to the wax lacquer.

very humid in China there were a couple of elements that had been affected by moisture that caused the pipes to split. We've just put the last replacement ones on there today. It's a bit of a blessing in disguise really because [the guys] have had no choice but to completely strip them, and now Kilvo knows every pipe. And they are better pipes now. We've got stuff from Hong Kong and Italy and the standards vary, not necessarily worse, just different."

Danny had been out to Italy a couple of times in the latter half of 2021 to see some of Franco's galvanics operations.

"I was gobsmacked by how much goes on over there. It's not known as an industrial or manufacturing place. Where the galvanics had been tested at a plant in the Alps, a magical medieval place, Varallo Sesia, about 20 miles from Switzerland and France that's ran by its own hydro-electric plant. We just walked out of the backdoor of the factory into this ancient town with a river and had coffee and pizza. We've got High Force Road cafe here! And, like everyone, the people were very helpful and want to see us succeed. We've had a couple of lads down today from Australia because they are buying some machines from Franco and came here to meet him and have a look and they are here for the next ten days. But even if someone wanted to set one up 10 miles down the road, we wouldn't say no at all, we'd encourage that. If anything, it would improve business, as it would definitely encourage people to use Middlesbrough as the country's pressing capital."

Danny is not wrong about Varallo Sesia. A beautiful enclave deep in the foothills of the Alps, famous for its churches and galleries, it was awarded the Gold Medal for Military Valour against the German occupation in World War II, and its Sacro Monte di Varallo pilgrimage site 150 metres above the town was included by UNESCO in the World Heritage List in 2003. Franco's Imprimatur Varade Vinili plant, located on the confluence of the Sesia and Torrente Mastallone, may look unassuming from the outside but inside the beautiful original brick arches have been respectfully refurbished and are vaguely reminiscent of Liverpool's Cavern Club, if it had windows all along one side. A quick look at the plant's Instagram account shows some striking similarities in the types of coloured and marbled vinyl the plant produces. On the surface it seems culturally and geographically worlds apart from Press On's Middlesbrough site – until one considers Middlesbrough's similarly proud heritage, and the homegrown ethos that both plants share.

With only five other pressing plants in the UK at the time of writing, and none further North than Market Harborough, Danny may well be onto something. As ever he was keen to take things one step further, with his vision post-Press On Vinyl imagining Middlesbrough as the vinyl capital of Europe: "All we've met are people trying to help and give us advice, and we want to do the same thing. In this industry there are so many different ways to do things, and it's a relatively old industry where people [are still taking] things from the 1950s to try, to people who are new to the industry in the last ten years. I read a study recently about streaming that more [money] goes into that, and vinyl is just to keep as a product, for collectors. I'm not saying that study is right, but a lot of industry also goes into big buildings full of servers, and streaming is throwaway. It's literally in one ear and out the other."

A lot has been written about physical product, and where the cassette revival stepped into the gap opened up by the vinyl supply problems, the CD revival may also be waiting in the wings. However, whatever your format of choice, the motivation is the same if slightly nuanced. Many people enjoy the thrill of the purchase or putting the physical product on to play for the first time; the crackle of the needle going down or the whirr of the CD. Others like something to hold while listening to the music. To me it's important to have something to read when I listen to something for the first time, so liner notes and CD booklets are an important part of the broader listening experience.

It all contributes to the uniquely personal experience of listening to music and is something that informs Press On Vinyl's commitment to all aspects of the production, delivery and customer experience of everything it has done and will come to do.

Returning to the pressing machines, I was keen to know how they ended up arriving on Christmas Eve after all, when the customs issues seemed sure to scupper a nice literary angle. Danny was still buzzing about it, explaining how they just kept chasing them to get them released and delivered on time. They had decided, as the machines weren't coming, they would have a Christmas party with a band and a DJ in the office on 23 December, but then the delivery company phoned and said the machines had been released after all and they could schedule them for delivery on Christmas Eve morning.

Danny: "So, we cancelled the band, and all went to bed at eight o'clock [laughs]! Christmas Eve was magic though, a few bleary eyes. And, because of that we were even in on Christmas Day because Man insisted, and we just unboxed the ornaments. Got our toys delivered a day early. I think everyone had the same feeling of just wanting to get back in..."

But it was not just the sight of physical machinery on the floor at this point that was motivating everyone. Back in the office, Emma was still flat-out all the time trying to work out shift patterns, as her role had grown to include admin, payroll and HR, and Tommy was similarly working pedal to the metal on FairSound. It was already obvious Press On Vinyl would have little need to self-promote in the traditional business sense; people had almost immediately started approaching them for records.

For visitors to the plant, the first thing they see is the open-plan office through the large double-fronted glass. On my many visits, I was nearly always met at the door with an enthusiastic and friendly welcome from whoever spotted me in the car park. With no reception area, you walk straight into the beating heart of Press On Vinyl operations. Toddy can often be seen, phone glued to his ear, to the left. Further up the office, Danny will be hunched over his laptop. To the right, Emma, Kerry and/or Gareth will be typing away. The décor is a colourful representation of the signage outside, nothing matches but there is a common contemporary but slightly retro style. As you might expect it is *very cool*.

But it's the far wall that has come to encapsulate the Press On Vinyl ethos for me. Floor-to-ceiling shelves filled with records, books and memorabilia that inform some of the company's social media, including the archetypal Press On Vinyl Stereo weekly playlist. Indeed, the actual turntable where all the listening and playbacks are done at this time takes pride of place in the centre of the shelves. A quick nose around sees Press On's tech of choice to be a Denon PMA-720AE amp powering a Technics SL-1210/mk2 turntable through some Acoustic Solutions AV-120 speakers.

So many people apparently turning up unannounced made every day exciting, Danny said. One fond recollection was of a Friday morning in June or July 2021 when the staff were all having a well-earned bacon sandwich break, and a couple in their sixties came to the door and introduced themselves as Winston and Rose from Brixton.

"Winston was logoed up and they have been running a reggae label for 40-odd years, Studio 16 with The Upsetters and Natty Dread, and they just wanted to come and meet us. They had set off from Brixton at 4am that morning. Lovely, lovely people. They are going to be one of the first things we press. Winston still releases a lot of independent reggae music. They came all that way, so we took them out for a meal on the night. When things like that happen, it does hit home how lucky we are. And, being a small independent label, they had all the same stories about being bumped to the back of the pressing queue."

By now Danny was on a roll and he could barely finish one sentence before starting the next. It was always exciting to see him so animated, as occasionally he seemed reserved, or even burdened – as if running a business, and what must also be a hugely stressful undertaking in the public eye, sometimes did get on top of him. However, when he was like this, he was a joy to talk to and I continued to be surprised sometimes at how upfront he was with me. "We have a consultant coming over from North America, which was one of the first things Toddy did, to sort that out. Obviously, we pay him, but we've never met him face to face yet. He has helped us set this plant up purely because Toddy searched the world for people in August 2020, and that is how we make our contacts. We always say we have a Toddy for that. He's like a shiny card or a top trump."

At this point, though, the company were about three months behind where they wanted to be. COVID had not helped with prices and logistics, and a shortage of the printed circuit board microchips that a lot of the plant's technology used compounded problems. There was also now a Polyvinyl Chloride (PVC) shortage (PVC being the material vinyl records are made from). Luckily they had stocked up two months in advance on the PVC pellets that are essential to producing the pucks that go on to become the records. "COVID also sharpened our minds," Danny told me.

Press On use raw virgin PVC pellets, and as part of the broader sustainability targets, they've recycled the vinyl offcuts and the trim since day one. Press On invested in a grinder very early on, which grinds the excess vinyl back into pellets. Any new mix can then include up to 15% recycled pellets. Only the centres of any unusable records are unable to be recycled, due to the way the labels fuse with the plastic in the pressing process.

"Back in Italy [at Franco's plant] they have what they call a special mix, which is all the colours mixed together. We are also in discussions with a company who believe they can turn recycled PVC back into virgin quality pellets. We are going to trial that for them and if it works, we will use that all the time. If it doesn't work, we will continue working towards it, because that is the future..."

In July, I followed this up with Toddy, as it sounded like a very interesting development. As much as Press On were attempting to do vis-à-vis sustainability, the pressing process creates a lot of wastage that is difficult to reduce beyond recycling the pressings that are not accepted and the trimmings from the successful cuts.

Although Toddy told me the trial had gone quiet, they were still up for taking part. Further ideas for reducing waste were being considered, while the company was also constantly on the look-out for more environmentally friendly production methods.

"Funnily enough last week I got an email about a new thing coming out. It's a brand-new company that are launching a new product at the beginning of September at the Making Vinyl Convention[16]. They've developed a new compound for making records that isn't PVC, and it's completely eco-friendly and used in sugar starches and stuff like that. Because it's made with bio products it's not as bad if it ends up in landfill, basically."

---

16 Making Vinyl Europe/Physical Media World Conference in Offenbach, Germany in 2022 was aimed at capitalising on the recent Recording Industry Association of America report that CDs and vinyl both showed growth together for the first time since 1996. The conference was to update the industry on similar European trends, with a goal to breathe new life into the packaged media industry. The second part, Making Vinyl Europe, concentrated on vinyl growth over the past 15 years.

The unnamed company had been testing the new product with GZ Vinyl in the Czech Republic, and at the most recent test, surface noise when the record was played back had been reduced to a level which made it acceptable to Press On's exacting quality control – if not yet quite as good as PVC vinyl.

The plan was for the new company to visit Press On in October 2022 to do some testing. It was a concern for Press On that the product was quite expensive, although this was mainly because it needed more financial backing in order to produce it on a bigger scale. It was working out at about £1.30 per unit, compared to less than 50p per unit for PVC.

Toddy continued: "If the quality is okay when it first goes out we will probably offer that [to artists] more expensively and with a caveat about surface noise. But as it gets better, one day, when PVC gets banned, at least there is a replacement that will be as good if not better. It's at a level now that most people wouldn't notice anyway. Most collectors wouldn't be bothered, but the absolute fanatics would. So that is dead exciting. The other thing we were meant to be a trial site for, but we never heard back. It sounds really good as well – the PVC is stripped back to its original compounds – but we will have to wait and see.

"At the minute we can grind up the flash [the edge wastage] and the purge [excess PVC from the extruder] and the waste records, but we do lose the centre [with the labels on] And we've [pressed records with] 100% regrind with the same stampers and then done blind testing here and most people picked the regrind.

"We've found by adding 50% regrind it stops a problem called non-fill which, depending on the heating and cooling times, can fluctuate anyway. [It's when] you sometimes get a funny shade on the record which you can physically see. It's caused when the stamper hasn't properly filled into the groove, particularly around the stamper edges, so the grooves aren't complete. Sometimes you can see it, but you can't hear it, and sometimes it sounds like it is missing frequencies, so there are obviously different levels of it. Now, with regrind, whether it is finer or been processed before, it gets rid of the shade."

Despite, or because, of this the guys sent the results of the regrind and a normal press to an expert mastering company we will hear more about later.

"Everything is subjective anyway, so even if they come back and say it isn't as good because of this, this and this, it would be great to know that there are technical reasons. But if people in the blind test think it is just as good then that is also great for us... And we've just had our first order for 100% regrind. Someone specifically asked for it for ethical reasons.

"We are always going to be putting 10-20% back in, because it seems to help the pressing and for business reasons it would be silly not to. PVC compounds have toxic additives to make it flow better and be stable. It isn't a throwaway plastic, so not as bad as clingfilm and things like that, but one day it could, and it does, end up in landfill, and that is not good for the environment so the more we can recycle for now the better."

Another reason why the bio-plastic development is a ground-breaking move. And while Toddy subconsciously downplayed the development, it sounded to me like a similar move to switching from 4-Star to unleaded petrol and, ergo, a pretty big deal...

The longer-term plans at the plant at this time were complex, large and progressive. An assessment had already been done on the roof of the building and, dependant on funding, the plan was to get solar panels on the whole of the roof. This would produce more electricity than they used at present, and enough to cover the extra presses they were expecting later in the year. The LPG gas the plant uses in the plumbing was already carbon offset, and they had already improved the pipes during the two-week shutdown, but Toddy was keen the work wouldn't stop there.

They had a generator for each pressing machine and were presently running both on one of the accumulator tanks. There would be some further rejigging of the pipes, so they would not need to purchase a new boiler for the two new presses and would continue to run off the existing set-up. The downside was that this would provide no leeway – if one boiler were to go down, they would lose two presses. However, by changing the pipework, the cooling would also be good enough for eight presses:

"When we can afford to, we will get one massive new boiler or a string of little ones and these will run the four presses plus another two. Six will be the ideal number in here. So that new boiler will run everything – and we are hoping, depending how much energy we have left over from the solar on the roof, we are either going to run it all electric and then sign up to renewable energy for the top-up electricity from the mains, which is probably more efficient. Or go for a hydrogen burner running green hydrogen.

"When we do that, which could be a year away, we will be powering all the electricity from this roof, all the steam from the green hydrogen boilers, and we could safely say that all our energy consumption is renewable. If that works, we can then say the records are completely eco-friendly – apart from maybe inks in printing but they are making progress there too," Toddy breathlessly told me, clearly invigorated at being able to find solutions in the industrial set-up of the plant, as well as the record pressing side itself.

Day 116
2 February 2022

The very first test presses came off the machines on 21 January, with Kilvo triumphantly holding one aloft on one of Kerry's Facebook posts. This was followed by the official Komparrison test pressings on Thursday, 27 January 2022, just in time for a private Press On Vinyl launch party the following day at a nightclub in nearby Stockton-on-Tees where the band performed live and a hundred-or-so specially invited guests partied the night away.

Far from the back-slapping corporate knees-up these events often are, the whole night was a very enjoyable celebration of what had happened so far. Kerry's mini-documentary had everyone watching engrossed, with huge cheers every time a colleague was featured, while a who's who of everyone from The Kids Are Solid Gold, *NARC Magazine*, Tees Music Alliance and many more of the region's music and culture influencers were on hand for a really positive night for Teesside, before Komparrison themselves took to the stage for a mixed set of their own stuff and some select covers.

As much as this was a great social occasion, if the Press On Vinyl story needs pinning from time to time, then this would definitely become one of the first significant pins. And they would soon be coming thick and fast as, on 8 February, the first test presses were sent out to paying customers...

As far as the public's perception of brand Press On goes, arguably the most important day of this first phase of the company's journey was on 2 February 2022, when the BBC cameras were on hand for the official turning on of the first pressing machine by saxophonist, filmmaker and all-round Teesside legend Yussef Nimer.

Yussef's story is quite something, and should be an inspiration to many first-generation immigrants that live in the cultural melting pot of Middlesbrough's Linthorpe Road area. Originally hailing from Dongola in Sudan, where the Blue Nile meets the White Nile, Yussef's dad got on a boat, ending up in post-war industrial Middlesbrough with no English and no passport.

A slight man, Yussef's father was approached by a local stevedore who, incredibly, introduced himself in their own dialect. The family moved to Liverpool, where the primary Sudanese community at the time was located, but with the steel boom still in full swing they soon moved back to Middlesbrough.

At that time, the Newport area near where the Press On plant is situated would have been a hive of cultures and creativity of varying degrees of legality. Born after his family arrived in the UK, young Yussef was an aspiring saxophonist.

He spent a lot of his time at the Jamaica Café, latterly the famous Bongo nightclub, as well as in the blues bars of nearby Gresham, where he honed his jazz credentials.

Prior work commitments meant I turned up just as the cameras were packing up but, clearly still on cloud nine, Danny regaled me of the morning's events: "Gary [Philipson] from BBC Tees and Lee Johnson from BBC were here for about three hours all together filming. It's going to go on to *Look North* and, if it's good enough, *BBC Breakfast*. They'll probably just wait for a slow news day!"

More importantly the whole process went well, with Danny taking the camera crews through every part of the pressing process even if he did joke that it made it look like they knew what they were doing.

And, increasingly, they did. Danny's almost constant self-effacement is another endearing trait for someone so outwardly confident, as he constantly seeks reassurances, like the cat who can't quite believe he got the cream. "Yussef pressed the button and the machine just kept churning them out."

Yussef would prove typically aloof when I tried to contact him for his memories of the day, but looking back over some video clips of the ceremony it is clear from his delight that he shares a similar pride in his adopted hometown, and we are reminded once again that Middlesbrough is a town built on immigration and innovation. With all Danny and Toddy's connections locally, and increasingly nationally (as well as Colin Oliver's myriad network), it might have been tempting to find somebody more high-profile for national press coverage – but Yussef epitomises the whole Press On ethos and, as such, was the perfect choice for the occasion.

As Danny was called away, Tommy concurred in the way I already knew Tommy would: "It's been all go this morning. Been churning them out like there's no tomorrow. Still test pressings, like. The second machine still needs a bit of calibrating. This one was doing three a minute all morning." Tommy gestured to the first machine, which now looked in need of some additional calibrating.

As much as the cameras captured a smooth button-pressing money shot which had then started an endless supply chain of vinyl production, as far as the armchair viewer was concerned, anyone who has ever worked in a factory knows this is not how production lines work. Although additional machines would later mean the plant would operate 24 hours a day, seven days a week, the parts, or all, of the machinery would need almost constant cleaning, maintenance and care in order to keep producing top quality records.

Danny and the others had always made that clear that Press On Vinyl would not just be about the ethos and the ethical angles, but that they also wanted to be the best. Which is why Franco, Man and the small select group of consultants were hired from the off.

Danny was suddenly back, gesticulating towards one of the pressing machines, chomping on a metaphorical apple so crisp it sounded like a desperate huntsman tramping through snow, such was the enthusiasm that still attached itself to every aspect of the Press On Vinyl project like the welks on the rusting Tuxedo Royale a mile or so away down river. With a perfectly timed, almost balletic, example of his every-day now, an engineer approached us with another virgin piece of silver-nitrate disc. "This is it, so what they are going to do now is put that stamper in that press, then we are going to get some test presses, pack them up and send them off to customers." As the engineer hands Danny another stamper he quickly looks it over, flips it between weathered hands and quips, "that will be unique that one with two B-sides, I like that."

With that little piece of showmanship, a subconscious reminder of who's boss perhaps, he suddenly remembers something else and goes digging around in a central row of crates that has been set up alongside the two pressing machines now they are producing more stock, before showing me another stamper. He holds it to the light and says, "this one is definitely EDM cos all EDM ones end up with this wavy pattern in the grooves and when you play it you can hear why it is patterned like that." It's an epiphany for me, as it had been for Danny one suspects, and that night I went home and thought about those repetitive patterns in the grooves and just for a moment it all made sense.

Day 140
26 February 2022

By mid-February the galvanics process was a lot more focused.

The Press On Vinyl galvanics lab is conspicuously in the middle of the factory floor, with a large window in the front so all can see the workers in lab coats and plastic goggles conducting their experiments. The lab is completely dust free, so stepping into the confined space through twin doors is something akin to boarding a submarine.

The complicated scientific process of creating the metal stamper to press the vinyl pucks into shape continued to amaze me, and how or why anyone thought to invent vinyl records 90 years ago. Luckily Beno was on hand with a ten-minute training session...

"So that was the master lacquer you saw there. It next goes in the silvering machine with all the silver nitrates and sodium hydroxides, which sprays it with a thin layer of silver before it goes in the pre-nickel bath, where it gets a very thin layer of nickel applied to it and that's the father. Then it goes in the other bath and when it comes out you can separate the two parts. The silver part is the mother, which you can use as a stamper. But if you are doing big runs, you'll need to put it back into the second deposition bath, and from the mother you will make three or four sons to do 2,000 to 3,000 records if you need to. The fathers and mothers will be stored away and then if anything needs repressing, they are still there, and everything is catalogued.

"Different recipes make different thicknesses. The mother needs to be quite fat so in ten years if someone wants another run, we can just pull that out and it will all sound exactly the same."

If that all sounds confusing, that's because it's an incredibly complex process. The wax master lacquer is what we often hear referred to as the master record, and that is used to create the stamper which presses the record out of a heated PVC puck.

At this stage Press On Vinyl hadn't received delivery of their lathe, so the master record was cut at a separate facility in Nottingham. The music is literally cut into the wax, hence the term cutting a disc. Once delivered to Middlesbrough, the galvanics team begin by washing the master disc and then spraying it with tin chloride and liquid silver before washing away any excess silver that doesn't attach. A duller metal is added to the silver side in bath one, which stiffens the disc ready for the electroplating process in bath two.

Electroplating simply involves immersing the silver-plated disc into a liquid tank of dissolved nickel, which then fuses with the silver surface through an electrical charge.

With the nickel now set into the grooves of the master record, the disc is removed from the electroplating tank and the metal layer is separated from the original lacquer disc, creating our 'mother', a mirror image of the lacquer, which can then be used to press the record. This is the mother stamper.

The stamper is polished using a backlapping machine so it is perfectly smooth, and then an optical centring punch is used to make a hole in the exact centre (+/- 0.1mm) before any excess metal is trimmed from the disc. To do this, a microscopic camera selects a groove as a focal point and as the stamper spins, the positioning of the stamper is adjusted so the camera is always pointed at the same groove until it's exactly centre and they can punch the hole.

Tommy is responsible for ensuring the centre labels are proofed and back from the printers in time, as they will fuse to the record as part of the pressing process. Once returned from the printer the labels are 'cooked' at low heat to ensure any moisture is removed as this can affect the pressing process, too.

Next the PVC pellets are hoovered into the hopper, a cannon-shaped machine that heats them to 320° Fahrenheit before feeding the liquid material into an extruder that condenses it into a small puck shape about the size of an ice hockey puck. This is fed into the 12" mould (or whichever size mould they choose to use) before being pressed, trimmed and cooled.

The pressing machine then holds the puck in place as the labels are placed above and below it before the stamper comes down at very high pressure to create a new vinyl record. Once cool, the excess vinyl is trimmed away. We now have a playable record.

As for the pressing machines themselves, they are each made up of these three parts: hopper, extruder and press. Each stamper, with a nominal maximum of 1,000 per stamp, can press at a speed of around 25 seconds per disc. The discs are then cooled very quickly to stop them bending.

The cooling process quickly seals in the stamp and the grooves that allow the record to be played before the hot plastic has any chance to degrade. It sounds so simple, but this is where Press On's complex plumbing set-up comes in. Located behind the breeze block wall, stretching two-thirds of the length of the factory floor, it would be explained to me in much more detail over the coming months, but I still struggled to fully comprehend some of the complexities of producing a record I can play at home.

Tommy: "There are two more pressing machines coming in May, but there is talk of them being sent as parts this time because there were so many niggling problems that we had to completely strip them and rebuild them anyway last time. The vinyl would come out lovely, but there would be a little 'v' shaped mark that wasn't meant to be there, which turned out to be a tiny bit of black vinyl left in the hopper. It's been a blessing in disguise really though. The guys know these machines inside out now. We're running a bit behind schedule but at least we know everything is going to be alright. We've already done a pink run, a little red run. We've been putting together test press packs and sending them out to clients. I come in here and some days these racks are full of vinyl."

As anyone with any engineering experience will know, these types of early teething problems and fine-tuning new machinery is all part and parcel of the job and, it's true, the pressing machines were being turned off a lot at this time.

But every problem solved at this stage was a time saver later, and once the plant was fully operational it had provided invaluable experience for the staff to really learn the inner workings of the machinery. The machinery would continue to be constantly cleaned, serviced and repaired anyway – one reason why securing Man's services early on was another of Toddy's inspired decisions.

FairSound was progressing quickly as well, if still in the background. Tommy summed it up succinctly, explaining how they had been sending the same back and forth emails to clients who initially requested high-end products before settling on plain black vinyl, and how that had become unnecessarily time consuming. They had finally built a menu guide over on the Press On website so that clients could do all the price comparisons themselves if they didn't like the original quote.

Tommy had also been busy finishing and proofing all the artwork, which was by now flooding in for the early pressings, and readying it all for the printers. The plan was eventually to print on site along with everything else, but they were currently using a number of printers for the sleeves.

Tommy: "Toddy is constantly on the phone to people about FairSound. We did an online demo [of the FairSound website] and it was lush. It still needs a bit of design work, but it won't be long until that is getting tested. We wanted it to be black and white [rather than the distinctive Press On Vinyl colours outside] so people can decorate it themselves, like MySpace. Unlike Facebook, you just have your own page, so you dive straight into your own shit. You'll have a sign-up page but once you're in, you're in. It's a lot like MySpace, but a lot more up to date. Facebook is difficult to navigate sometimes, and you don't know what you're looking at."

For those too young to remember, or those that hoped to forget, MySpace's early incarnation allowed users to really express themselves by being able to modify profiles so much more than the generic themes offered by the likes of Facebook and WordPress. It was a place where making friends was easy and trolls were absent. Some of this might be rose-tinted spectacles but listening to Tommy talk about how he hopes Toddy's vision for FairSound might reinvigorate music-based social media is a tonic, if worryingly unlikely with similar retail platforms already being offered by Rough Trade, Norman Records and any other indie distributor with a message board. But this is something we would revisit in a lot more detail later.

I finally managed to pin Danny down for 20 minutes (finding him engrossed in conversation deep along the corridor of complex plumbing works, a kind of industrious Upside Down to the creative manufacturing of the pressing and galvanics side) if initially still a little distracted by the plumbing issues. "We've just been getting more test presses out the door really to get verified and approved."

Last time I'd caught up with Danny, he told me he wanted to be running the plant 24 hours a day, seven days a week by now: "Yeah, nowhere near."

The plant was now running at 16 hours a day, five days a week. This had been successfully rolled out in the previous few weeks, but Danny thought it was unlikely they would be going fully 24/7 until at least the middle of March. They were now pressing 400 to 500 records a day, which was also a lot less than they wanted to be doing at this stage. Mainly still test presses as they continued to perfect the product, with many getting ground down and recycled. Danny had arranged for some of the test presses to be inspected by a very high-end cutting and mastering studio in London, Curved Pressings[17], who gave Press On a comprehensive report. Of the five test presses they submitted, two were borderline for a couple of reasons but nothing major, two were good and one was extremely good.

"Everything is prep. More time to prep, we don't need to rush the prep. Obviously when the machines are going that is quite a quick thing so it's all about cleaning and preparing, whether it is the lacquers or the stampers, or the presses themselves. Sometimes dust causes golf ball-style dimples so we are inspecting them all *at the moment*." Danny hands me a defective stamper. "We are just perfecting it, but you can see the mark on the side of this one, and if you hold it up to the light you can see a dent in it, but the sound quality is definitely there. The staff are getting better every day."

In fact, more people had been offered jobs, but weren't being given start dates until Danny and Toddy were confident they could train them to the required standard. "If we bring them in too early, when we are still finding our feet as well, it's not a great environment to put them in with too many variables. FairSound is on the back burner and won't be getting beta-tested until April, but we are sponsoring NXTGN Festival."

NXTGN was a sister festival to Middlesbrough's Twisterella and was due to take place in March. Ultimately, it was cancelled due to poor ticket sales as local shows struggled to rebuild post-COVID confidence. The sponsorship using

---

17   Curved Pressings is a vinyl and CD mastering and manufacturing company based in Hackney. It was founded in 2000. The operation was previously a pressing plant with a galvanics department and is the sister company of the vinyl record cutting, mastering and recording studio Curve Pusher.

the FairSound brand was intended to be the start of Press On rolling FairSound out to artists, as the NXTGN promoters were known to really promote up and coming acts. But the fact the festival (and the sponsorship) failed to materialise was perhaps a blessing in disguise as, in hindsight, FairSound was not quite ready at this stage. However, the plan to give all the artists on the bill a test pack with more information, bits of merchandise and offers of tours around the plant was something they would come close to revisiting when FairSound finally did sponsor a local stage at Twisterella Festival in October 2022.

Danny would often say that there was lots of other exciting stuff he couldn't really tell me about. This became something of a recurring theme on my visits, as each time I arrived he fed me little clues of things they would announce in the coming weeks. If annoying it did, at least, allow me to second-guess and plan around things, such as a very high-profile visit to the site that might or might not happen. On that occasion it didn't, but the reality was things were moving so fast at this time that plans changed from one day to the next. Ideas were formulated and rejected, rolled out and changed, as everyone learned what was working and what wasn't.

"We've had a lot of exposure from the BBC." *Look North* and *BBC Breakfast* both picked up on the relatively low-key launch event, repeating the broad narrative of the time that the plant hoped to press 50,000 records per month in order to part-fill the market gap caused by the continued surging demand for vinyl. They mentioned Adele and Fleetwood Mac. *Look North* also shoehorned in a Sam Fender mention, as is their wont.

Danny was no stranger to being in the spotlight. Back in 2019, he had appeared on *Look North* to recite the poem that appears at the beginning of this book and so perfectly encapsulates the pride he and his colleagues share in their local area. "So, all that has led to some higher-profile people reaching out to us. We are going to be doing some interesting releases over the course of the summer. The first release will be Komparrison on 11 March, so we will press the limited print run by 4 March to get it in the shops for the 11th. 500 [records] in total: 200 on pink vinyl, which are the ones people have pre-ordered, and then we'll have the rest in shops at higher prices because people get something for pre-ordering. Then a further 300 black..."

I suppose at this point we might be wondering how an alarm fitter and a foyboat skipper came to manage one of the most anticipated local EP releases of the year on exclusive limited vinyl, from their own pressing plant, as a way of flagshipping their unique take on a global problem? The simple mundane fact is that they have help, a lot of it – and admittedly some of the best help in the world.

Right at the start of the Press On Vinyl idea, Toddy had scoured the internet searching for an expert consultant in setting up this kind or endeavour. While the consultant he found declined to be involved or named for this book due to his other business interests, he comes with an international pedigree. Now based in North America, he previously worked out of South East Asia as a sort of central base to reach a diaspora of jobs.

What Toddy could tell me was: "He's been our consultant all the way, since we first conceived the idea. September 2020, he started working with us, but because of COVID the first time we could get him over here was late February. But the whole team corresponds with him every day, whatever we need to know from a logistics point of view, pressing point of view… He's set pressing plants up all over the world. He's well versed, a good guy, fun as well, and he wants to continue to be involved going forward." Enough to confirm that Press On Vinyl will only work with people who fit into their ethos, and that very much includes the prerequisite of being 'fun'.

Andy Knight is another example of the help they receive. He's an engineer who works over the road from Press On Vinyl, at The Welding Institute. Danny told me Andy had been giving Press On Vinyl almost constant support and advice in his own time, so whenever the team hit a problem they have that technical reassurance as part of a local goodwill network.

"We needed to modify one part of the machines and that was turned round in a day. Also, we've still got Man and he'll be here until we are properly up and running. He's got the Hong Kong issue, with family over there, but he's got British Overseas Citizenship so he's going to come over here to live – another quirky by-product of the whole thing…"

Press On Vinyl's political position, while not particularly radical in the grand scheme of things, seemed to have ruffled a few feathers, though, with them being cast as some sort of socialist outlier in an almost psycho-capitalist industry. A raisin in a sea of curry sauce.

It's easy to make light (or otherwise) of stunts like the Cuban flag on the outside of the building, but Danny's genuine interest in Man's family situation came from a deep-rooted need to share what he has and to help others whenever he can. And, as a footnote of sorts, it should be noted the Cuban flag still remains gently wafting in the rafters at the far end of the warehouse, if you take the time to look up from the industrious scenes on the floor.

Finding myself roughly halfway through the reporting period of this book, I also thought now would be a good time to ask Danny where he predicted Press On Vinyl would be by October 2022, at the end of their first year in business.

"I'd like to think we'll be four machines 24/7, so now let's see how the book ends. I might be back in my fire-alarm job!"

We've already touched on Press On Vinyl's prehistory, and it is inconspicuous to say the least. Before the start of this book, before Danny and Toddy even got the keys to the empty warehouse…

Danny told me: "We had our own label, Goosed Records and we tried to get a record pressed. It was a grass roots label aimed at grass roots artists. We never made any money from it but then we tried to get a compilation album made for the label with ten artists we had released. That was in September 2019. The lead times were ridiculous, and there was no guarantee we would have got them before Christmas to release. As a label we'd only ever released stuff digitally before."

It always goes back to a pint in a pub, doesn't it?

"So many conversations about it, some in the pub, some not. Then Toddy researching and researching and researching saying, 'I've seen this. Have you looked at this? Can we do this?'. Then we looked at what we could achieve in this area with the investment that is going on here [at TeesAMP], tied everything together, and it just snowballed. Middlesbrough, initially, but then specifically this area. When we get visitors, they are surprised. They think it's going to be some poky, dingy warehouse and it's absolutely not, so that is something we are really happy with. And I can walk here from home!"

The industrial park itself is a brand new development, made up of similar looking cube-shaped buildings, all very clean and spacious, and part of Tees Valley Combined Authority's continued plans to redevelop the old industrial plains along the River Tees.

As well as grants and favourable rates for new businesses, the plans also included a controversial freeport and further development around Middlesbrough Football Club's Riverside Stadium, which previously failed to take off.

As far as TeesAMP goes, at the time of writing, it was still unfinished and only partly occupied – but from an arterial dual carriageway into the park, Press On Vinyl's distinctive colours are visible as soon as you enter.

Other innovation-based manufacturing businesses in the first wave of occupation included an engineering company that created over 100 new jobs, and by October 2021 there was just one empty unit remaining. By June 2022, building work would recommence on the site and more units were starting to spring up. Danny told me they were very keen for Middlesbrough Council to support his mission around sustainability, especially regarding putting solar panels on all the new buildings. A longer-term goal was to secure funding as a collective of businesses to utilise the nearby River Tees.

It was difficult to imagine Press On Vinyl being anywhere else, not just geographically in the North, in Teesside or in Middlesbrough, but on this specific site, and in that particular plot. Destiny, perhaps, and something Danny would later unknowingly connect the dots to when he told me about a network of underground railway lines Father of Railways George Stephenson helped design very close to, if not on, the actual site of the Press On Vinyl building.

Danny also spoke about an event he called Free Independence Day, which he hoped to put on over the summer, to celebrate all the independent record shops, promoters and labels in the area and, most importantly, the local music scene.

While it initially sounded like the name came first, he envisioned a decent-sized event with a record fair at Middlesbrough Town Hall Crypt, a much under-used room underneath the famous main room, with a gig in the even more under-appreciated courtyard. We chatted for a while about the excitement of going down the steps into cellar venues, and about a night Goosed Records used to put on, Club Spadger, in another legendary Middlesbrough venue called Purple Onion.

"Goosed is now mainly to support everything else and to point people in the right direction. We will still put some stuff on in Sticky Fingers, but we've handed it over to some younger promoters. I'd love to think there will still be a Goosed vinyl at some point. Just before COVID, for Independent Venue Week, we had some gigs on at Sticky's all week, but on the Thursday we did an unplugged night which was recorded and we might put that down on a vinyl. Eight different bands and with it all being recorded in one night the levels will be fairly even, so it will transfer to vinyl quite easily, I think. There is something about compilation albums. Quintessentially grassroots."

While Free Independence Day never materialised, it was another example of Danny's seemingly unquenchable thirst for all things local music. Even as the company was becoming increasingly high profile, the director still had one eye firmly on the music scene it was initially conceived to support and would continue to inspire, no doubt. As I got to know more about the business, though, I realised that no idea was ever completely abandoned. So while Free Independence Day didn't happen in 2022, never say never.

Around this time rumours persisted that some local acts from yesteryear who had never been able to release their albums on vinyl might get the chance to. These particularly surrounded Henry Carden's Dartz!, who are something of a local musical touchstone having had a modicum of success nationally after the release of their debut album, *This Is My Ship*, in 2007. And partly because of guitarist Henry's almost guaranteed involvement in anything exciting happening music-wise in Middlesbrough or Stockton. In fact, some of my more tangential conversations with Danny and Toddy often leant towards Press On Vinyl acting as much like a label as a pressing plant, though they always distanced themselves from that if questioned directly. "I think periodically we might pick some legacy artists that had some exposure, but have been forgotten about a bit. Space Raiders[18] is one I've been trying to reach out to. Werbeniuk is another…"

---

18   Space Raiders were big beat also-rans signed to Fatboy Slim's Skint Records label. Keener-eyed Teesside music fans will know the group originated in Middlesbrough after being formed by ex-Shrug drummer Gary Bradford.

While any, or all, of these names might be largely forgotten in the grand scheme of things, their small part in the industry should not be downplayed. If there is demand for even a small run of vinyl, then that fits the Press On Vinyl remit perfectly, while also potentially keeping the machines pressing should any downtime or gaps in the diary appear further down the road to validation.

Day 166
24 March 2022

On 11 March 2022, Komparrison's debut EP *You Say She's Satisfied* was released on all the usual streaming services but, more crucially, on beautiful bespoke vinyl in a limited run of 200 pink and 300 black discs. They sold out almost immediately.

Just like that Press On Vinyl were in business.

It was not only the first record released and pressed at Press On Vinyl, and in Middlesbrough itself, but also the first to be pre-ordered and sold via the FairSound landing page. It felt like validation for everything Danny and the team had been saying for all those months: concrete, tangible, and gloriously camp proof that Press On Vinyl was for real.

The day itself was unremarkable. The two presses whirred and stamped throughout, mostly without incident. In the lab, Franco and young protegée Emily Skipper continued to perfect their solution recipes. Emily would also be interviewed for Women In Vinyl[19], where she waxed lyrical about her role within the company and how she came to work there.

In the evening, the occasion was marked with a special launch event at Middlesbrough's Bad Neighbour Records. Adjoining Sticky Fingers Bar on Linthorpe Road (not to be confused with the similarly named Sticky's in Stockton), since opening and installing their own baby grand piano amongst the vinyl crates, it had become something of a spiritual second home for the Press On Vinyl team.

As the only vinyl stockist in Middlesbrough besides HMV, Bad Neighbour was also the Press On team's first port of call to see the Komparrison disc in the racks alongside all their favourite records, from the Strokes to Wolf Alice to, yes, Adele. Komparrison then performed a stripped back set of tracks from the EP. It was fitting that the venue originally intended as the home for Danny and Toddy's Goosed Records before the pandemic caused a drastic rethinking by the owners (as we will hear more about later) would still play a small part in their new

---

19 'Emily Skipper | Galvanics, Press On Vinyl', 2 April 2022, https://womeninvinyl.com/2022/04/02/emily-skipper-galvanics-press-on-vinyl/. Women In Vinyl was created in 2018 by Jenn D'Eugenio, who works as the sales and customer service manager at Furnace Record Pressing in Alexandria, Virginia. It is a blog, website and online community showcasing women working in the industry by sharing their stories with the world. Its mission statement is to empower women, female-identifying, non-binary, LGBTQ+, BIPOC and otherwise marginalised humans working in the industry to create, preserve and improve the art of music on vinyl.

lives. The showcase was to be the first Sticky Fingers live music tie-in.

With the business now starting to recoup their not-insubstantial outlay I started to wonder more about other pressing plants and how they operate. What I quickly discovered was opaque business models, small print hidden away in FAQ tabs, and no obvious price plans – something that started to feel increasingly like hoop-jumping for clicks, the further into websites I went. Not something that was helpful or beneficial to small artists, those on a limited budget, or those taking their first daunting steps towards releasing a record...

In terms of the Press On Vinyl ethos, I've written a lot about how the business was built on a unique ethical foundation in a famously greedy and cut-throat industry, so I decided to look at another pressing plant with a similar forward-looking social media presence. One that had started conspicuously showing up on my Facebook feed as hints of bandwagon-jumping were starting to appear within the industry.

On the surface, Diggers Factory in Toulouse is another pressing plant looking to modernise and distance themselves from traditional vinyl production. Crucially, their mission statement says they will allow "any artist, label or producer" to book a slot. This can be taken a number of ways, but when taken literally, is a very different ethos, even if they are similarly claiming to be changing the system. While their position on overproduction and waste, on-demand production, and small-run capabilities is to be admired, the disclaimer allows for a cash injection from a major label if needed – whereas Press On Vinyl have made it clear they will not be tying up schedules based on financial clout. (In fact, 16-week premium slots would be offered almost as standard by many pressing plants across Europe by the end of 2022.)

At first glance the Diggers Factory set up is very similar to that at Press On. Their 12- to 18-week lead time is only activated when a pre-order threshold is reached. Any shortfall in funding, and the project is cancelled with all parties reimbursed, something FairSound would mirror when the crowdfunding part of the platform was launched.

Diggers Factory, at least on their website, is much less personable than Press On. Even the language they use is almost apologetic about the lead times, as if sensing their own shortcomings in customer service, finishing one soundbite paragraph with "then, you'll have to wait 12 to 18 weeks for manufacturing, before we ship the records to your contributors." To give them the benefit of the doubt though, some meaning may literally be lost in translation.

For direct comparison purposes, let's remember that FairSound planned to incorporate crowdfunding into Press On's 16-week lead time, and the trigger point for production (or the Press On Point) was first planned to be when 65% of the total funding had been reached. This was later removed all together.

Importantly, on closer inspection, like many companies offering pressing capacity to artists, it is literally just that. Diggers Factory has capacity at external pressing plants, while mastering and distribution is also outsourced. Its online community is little more than a blog, with a lot of information buried away in an FAQ tab.

We might start to imagine a more pyramid shape to the usual vinyl pressing set-up where large warehouses of pressing machines churn out commercial orders without any further thought for the product or artist.

It now starts to make a lot of sense why not only having their own pressing plant on-site, but also outsourcing as little as possible, immediately puts Press On in a much stronger position. Not only in guaranteeing delivery, but also in not having to purchase capacity elsewhere.

By contrast, the unnamed plant in London I mentioned in the Prologue, which gave over full capacity to a similarly unnamed major label, was thriving. It had one of each model of the three Neumann lathes. It also had a similar straight-to-lathe concept offering the fully analogue experience Press On hoped to provide, where the music would be recorded, mixed and mastered in real-time as the lathe cut the lacquer. The method is widely regarded as the best, way to record vinyl and produces the smooth, warm sound vinyl fanatics argue cannot be replicated on other formats – although there is some dispute as to the actual definition of live-to-lathe, which would mar even Jack White's Third Man set-up. Even slight delays in mastering, favoured by White to minimise the chance of mistakes, is considered not to be in the purist spirit of the concept dating back to the Memphis and Detroit heyday.

The version of live-to-lathe at Press On would require a producer to literally mix live. If they operated it that way, it would be a world first. Press On would later claim to be the only plant in the world offering the format without using magnetic tape or digital storage.[20]

In June 2022, in an interview with *Ultimate Guitar* website[21], Jack White waxed lyrical (as it were) about his live-to-acetate concept being intimidating for artists, but there was no mention that it might also be intimidating for producers, or of whether a digital safety net might also be in use.

The London plant was fully set-up to produce 12" and 7" stampers in their own galvanics lab, with the whole thing slickly soundbitten together on an equally sleek-looking website. Tellingly, the company has on-site printing facilities for a truly end-to-end service. If we look at things completely from a business perspective, why shouldn't they give over full capacity for a guaranteed financial position? It's just two different methods with the same end result, sort of. Morally, well, you decide…

---

20   Toddy later hatched a bizarre plan to break Jack White's 2014 world record for the fastest studio-to-store record. Toddy thought they could shave just over 30 minutes off the previous record of 3 hours 55 minutes – even talking about shipping it along the Tees (Sex Pistols fashion, in order to avoid traffic) to Sound It Out Records in Stockton, where the historic sale would take place. The idea at the time was to get Middlesbrough Asylum Project to record the audio. The constantly evolving ensemble incorporates a lot of different cultures and is very comfortable with a bit of improvisation.
21   'Jack White Explains Why Some Musicians Can't Handle "Bizarre" Scenario of Recording Live-To-Acetate at His Third Man Records', The Phoenician, 24 June 2022, https://www.ultimate-guitar.com/news/general_music_news/jack_white_explains_why_some_musicians_cant_handle_bizarre_scenario_of_recording_live-to-acetate_at_his_third_man_records.html

In 2018, Liverpool's Jacaranda Records had also started offering, on their website, a much more streamlined version of both Press On's and Diggers Factory's processes, with less artist involvement.[22]

The Jacaranda name can be traced all the way back to the late 1950s, when Allan Williams opened his café on Slater Street. It soon became central to the Merseybeat scene, hosting early performances by the likes of Gerry and the Pacemakers, Rory Storm and The Silver Beetles. The venue has continued to function as a label and music venue and, in 2018, announced it was branching out into vinyl pressing.

The company's main selling point was their immersive audio capability, which claims to give the listener complete 360-degree sound (experienced in full via headphones) and was widely adopted by mega-corporations such as Netflix, Apple and Sky. However, when I contacted Jacaranda Records with an enquiry about a short run vinyl reissue, here is the reply I received:

"Thanks for your email. Although we had plans a few years ago to move into vinyl production, the crazy events of the past few years have put paid to that for a little while. We run a small record label, three music venues, a pub, a night club, a record store and an events and bookings company but currently no vinyl plant."

(See next page for QR code.)

---

22 'Liverpool opens first vinyl pressing plant in 30 years', Richard Smirke, 17 December 2018, https://www.bigissuenorth.com/news/2018/12/liverpool-opens-first-vinyl-pressing-plant-30-years/

Day 178
5 April 2022

When I first met Danny in autumn 2021, his vision for Press On Vinyl seemed like a loose coalescence, or at least a coalition of disparate ideologies and ideas all jockeying for dominance. FairSound was over there, the galvanics operation was isolated in its little lab, and the pressing machines were down there. All valid enterprises, but without the acumen that would hold them all together. Now, almost six months later in late March 2022, Danny is a man who definitely has all his ducks in a row. I started hearing more concise and more business-like talk of different departments within the company structure, which immediately sounded more organised and premeditated.

A further £350,000 of investment from FW Capital Debt Finance, part of the Northern Powerhouse Investment Fund (NPIF), had been secured to help support working capital requirements, which would help generate and sustain at least 39 new jobs at the plant.

There was also a two-week shutdown planned in April. The shutdown was initially required because the steam traps that separate the water from the steam before it is piped through to the pressing machines had to be completely replaced, as water had started to seep through. But the two weeks would also allow the team to build a fully sound-proofed recording studio and install the new £180,000 lathe, integral to the end-to-end ethos of the company. The plan was to build an extension to the office space and unfinished mezzanine level. The mastering suite and live room would offer same-day studio-to-vinyl services on site, another first in the UK. At this point it was only described as 'microphone-to-vinyl in a day', but it was a concept that would allow artists to take their records home with them on the same day.

The shut-down would ensure the dust-free conditions of the plant weren't compromised, and when I spoke to Danny, he was adamant this development had always been part of the Press On Vinyl vision.

Back out on the factory floor, Beno was fastidiously checking and sleeving a batch of 500 Charlie Simpson white vinyls to make sure there were no black smudges in the plastic caused by a dirty extruder. Tommy shouted me over to have a look at the new wall of shame, which served as a constant reminder to the factory staff of the sort of problems to look out for.

Rejected records with smudges, scratches and square edges (where the puck wasn't correctly aligned) adorned the breeze blocks in the corner where the factory floor listening station was located. Some had obvious faults that wouldn't necessarily affect the quality of the sound, while others had near-invisible imperfections, but with catastrophic impacts on the sound when played back. For Press On Vinyl, any error is an error. The perfectionist approach is another thing that sets the company apart from most other pressing plants.

I was immediately drawn to a beautiful blue and white splatter disc: the Low Hummer album, released on 8 April on Dance To The Radio, and the second release from the Press On Vinyl floor. Tommy explained that in order to get the unique effect they had to heat the blue and white PVC pellets separately. The blue went through the hopper and extruder as normal, but the white had to be heated more slowly, before each blue puck was manually placed in the pressing machine with some of the white pellets and pressed that way. While this process creates completely unique individual discs, it's time consuming and laborious for the engineers manually operating the press. With only two pressing machines available, it would be some time before the plant agreed to make any more discs of this nature.

Tommy: "So, they had to get a slow cooker from Currys and then warm all the white pellets in it. Then every time a blue puck came through, they had to pepper it with white pellets just in time for the stamper to come down. There was 400 to 500 of them. I don't know whose idea it was, a process of elimination, I think. It wasn't smooth sailing, I know that. Only the pellets touching the bowl in the slow cooker get hot so if you put too many in they get too claggy and all stick together."

Pete Haste, engineer: "You can run the pressing machine manually, or auto, or semi-auto, so we did the white pellets in semi-auto but it took a few goes to get it right. The white pellets weren't as hot as the blue, so if there was one on the edge it would chip off." Indeed, holding up one of the earlier botched vinyls to the light you can clearly see the profile of the while pellets against the blue vinyl, so while the splatter effect looks sublime to the cursory eye, the technical know-how (or not-so-known-how) is also evident if you know what to look for. "We'll not do any more of them for a while!"

Tommy gestured to the slow cooker. In the same corner, there was an industrial fan oven being used to dry some labels for future vinyl presses. To the untrained eye the space looked like a normal work breakout area, but to Press On Vinyl it had become something of an off-piste workaround base where everyday items could be seen fixing complex engineering complications. The labels, for example, have to be completely dry before they go onto the puck, or they can tear or crease.

Tommy confirmed FairSound website was getting closer to being ready and the site configurator was just about up and running. It should allow users to get a 3D image of the products they were browsing. Then all the orders would go through the website rather than everything being done by email, which had been taking up valuable man hours – especially with the orders now coming in thick and fast. The Press On Vinyl website was already getting over 500 visits per week, with the majority of people logging on for over a minute. This was a big deal at the time, by all accounts. With the normal website being that popular, it was projected that FairSound could be up to ten times busier.

Press On had initially hired a third-party developer to manage FairSound, but the results weren't always agreeable to both sides. In the end, Danny decided to bring in another mate who was able to set up the configurator within a few days, with an excellent outcome. The configurator basically allowed anyone accessing the site to get a quote and would eventually be launched on the Press On Vinyl website (not FairSound) on 30 March. Kerry, in her new role of Visual Director, was also doing all the social media side of things. All the increasingly detailed videoblogs alongside the easily digestible meet-the-team features were her work. This allowed Hanglands, who had been working on the social media aspect, to focus on FairSound, which had always been the intention. However, in the coming months FairSound would become something of a headache as Danny and Toddy struggled to reconcile the platform with their original vision.

Upstairs, the breakout room was almost finished, with the usual kettle and sink (the stairs still slightly sticky with wet paint), complete with old stampers doubling as artwork on the walls and a couple of stylish floor-to-ceiling windows looking down over the factory floor – a constant reminder of where you were.

"Still no dartboard!" Tommy remonstrated, before immediately redeeming himself: "It will be a mint view from here when there are five or six machines all going. Imagine four more machines and another two or three packers, but it wouldn't need to be more hectic. Lush, man."

A tired matter-of-factness seemed to overcome him, and I wondered what really brought him here. What roundabout route led him to his dream job when so many never get to have a satisfying occupation, never mind one they genuinely thrive off? As we cast our eyes over the scene below, Tommy became quite reflective, as if the perspective allowed him to briefly remember how lucky he was to be involved in such an astonishing project from such humble beginnings, with the slow cooker still in view.

"The pressing machine on the right has been named Tex after our friend, and the machine on the left is called John Paul, after our mate Johnny. Both of them are unfortunately dead, but they would work here if they weren't, simple as that. Tex played bass in Middlesbrough for years. He was older when he died – but Johnny was only our age." There is an ageless quality to Tommy's look and manner, so let's hedge and say he means late thirties. "His family all came down and formally opened the machine for us. It was a good day that, really nice." The two machines were formally named on 24 February, with the first pink Komparrison coming off the John Paul press on 7 March. This wasn't down to chance. It was a tender moment, but also another notch on the philanthropy bedpost for the company. This attention to even the minutest detail would become just another thing that set Press On Vinyl apart from other pressing plants, no matter how much they might start trying to match them in the coming months.

Danny liked to talk about the success stories of the staff not just commercially; he often stressed the human successes of some of the staff who had previously been down on their luck or had less stability in their lives. While an accomplished designer, Tommy's background is like something from a Boy's Own story. He may not have met Danny in the metaphorical sandpit, but it wasn't far off. "I was a rope access technician for 15 years before doing this – a steeplejack, basically, working all around the globe, but before the lads could finish explaining their plan for Press On Vinyl I was in up to me chin and quit my old job the very next day.

"I first met Danny when I sat next to him in class at school in first year and since that very first minute together, we've spent the last 30 years pissing our pants laughing. We grew up together; moved in together; formed a band, The Danny Kebabs, together. Danny's Nana fed me most nights growing up, under the proviso that I could only come back the next night if I finished my plate. I met Toddy when I was in my early twenties, when our group of mates united slap bang in the middle of the notorious Ben's Biggun." Who and what Ben's Biggun is/was shall remain unrecorded on this occasion.

An even more uplifting story is Sweetie's (Andrew Sweeting, Packing & Logistics). The vinyl fanatic had been down on his luck, out of work and living at his dad's after splitting from the mother of his daughter. With a background in care and bar work, and a singular love for vinyl records, he was unsure what to do with himself when Toddy called. On top of all this, Sweetie had been recovering from a bad accident which had left him with metal plates in both his ankles and had even been in a wheelchair for a time.

Sweetie: "I've collected records since I was about 14 and knew Danny and Toddy from going to see bands. It couldn't have come at a better time. I'd just broke up with my missus, was living at my dad's and I didn't have a clue what to do with myself work-wise after the accident. Toddy rang me and told me about Press On because he thought I would be ideal for checking the records because I spend a lot of time at home doing that anyway! I knew about warps and how to tell if a record is off-centre, but there was a lot of stuff I didn't know about how it's caused so I've learnt a lot.

"People kept saying 'What are you going to do?' and I just wanted to do something I like with records, but everyone said I wasn't being realistic. I've done support work and bar work in the past but never found what I really wanted to do. I get distracted very easily but here, I want to stay here for the rest of my life.

"I liked doing support work, it was nice helping people, but it's great here, it's a good atmosphere. It brings you up. They've even helped with flexitime for my daughter. She lives in Scarborough, but they realise family is important, which makes things easier outside of work." It's difficult not to be drawn in by Sweetie's gentle loyalty and endearing disposition to his friends, which couldn't be further from Danny's ebullient embrace. But that is why Danny visibly fizzes with excitement when he talks about these recruitment successes being more than technical- or career-minded. In a worst-case scenario, Sweetie could have become lost in a system of ever-decreasing benefits and return-to-work interviews, further disconnecting him from occupational fulfilment.

Still up in the mezzanine, and as if suddenly pulling back from too much of a Proustian moment, Tommy noticed someone on the factory floor taking pictures.

"That's Alex Balzama. This mezzanine floor is his baby. He's got his own online studio in North Yorkshire, but he is going to set up the studio here and run it on a part-time basis, on-call if needed. Toddy is good at that, too, which is how he got into all of this in the first place. They were on about putting it somewhere else off-site, which would have meant a group of lads having to leave here to work there..." That sadness again, at the thought of seeing his friends and colleagues having to work on another site, just strengthens the sense of camaraderie and another intangible force driving the Press On Vinyl project.

As we spoke Danny was meticulously preparing a £250,000 lacquer for silvering. The lacquer would be used for a 250-run Pete Townsend pressing with artwork by Damien Hirst, to be auctioned off at £1,000 each for Cancer Research. Danny was carefully sanding the positive and negative anode and cathode sides of the Pete Townsend lacquer to expose the metal at the centre in order to create the charge that will form the stamper and ultimately press the records. I watched the lacquer be successfully silvered and immersed first in one tank to produce the unique father, and then into the slightly cooler ionised tank to produce the mother, which would be used to produce multiple son stampers, if required. Music – in this case very expensive music – being created, literally, before my eyes.

With the sanding complete Danny talked me through the process in his inimitable 13-to-the-dozen way, as the charity disc first went into the silvering machine...

Danny: "So this is the silvering machine... give it a rinse... putting the first layer of silver on the lacquer which makes it conductive... it then goes in the baths and this will make the father... it's quite solid but you can't touch the silver or it will rub off. This is the start of growing the stamper and once you've started you really need to keep it wet as you are growing something electrically[23]... If we need to do more

---

23   Galvanics part 1: Once the lacquers are cut, they go through the galvanics process which starts with a silver spray being applied to the lacquer. 'Silvering' is where the lacquer is placed on a slowly rotating vertical turntable and sprayed with a very fine silver nitrate spray. This penetrates the lacquers' grooves with exact accuracy and prepares it with a metal surface ready for the electro-plating process. For the electroplating you are in fact plating the disc using electrolysis. Electroplating, also known as electrochemical deposition, is a

than a thousand we make a mother and make a copy of the father, and with that mother you can make a lot of sons... you can't make any more of the lacquer because it is wax and it degrades.

"We'll keep the lacquer for about three months, because we have been known to use them twice, and for reference, in case there are any issues from the customer with the test press... For this Damien Hirst one, the lacquer and the stampers will be worth a fortune, though. If I was them, I'd have the stampers framed to auction off."

The Pete Townsend disc had just been submerged for vacuum deposition. The second bath is at a lower temperature. The recipe is very similar but ramped up incrementally to 140 amps, where it stays for an hour as the father is created.[24]

---

process for producing a metal coating on a solid substrate through the reduction of cations of that metal by means of a direct electric current. The part to be coated acts as the cathode (negative electrode) of an electrolytic cell; the electrolyte is a solution of a salt of the metal to be coated; and the anode (positive electrode) is usually either a block of that metal, or of some inert conductive material. The current is provided by an external power supply. So, the lacquer is placed in a salt solution bath where during this chemical process the nickel builds up on the disc where it fills the grooves and creates an image of that lacquer which is then carefully separated and used to press the record itself, one for each side of the record. It's possible to do a multiple step process that creates backups of that lacquer if you do larger runs of that record. The first part of the process creates a 'mother' which is the backup of the master and can create seven or eight stampers while the second bath creates a 'father' which is a backup of the backup master. The stampers are essentially a reverse image of the master's record grooves and are then used to press the actual records.

24   Galvanics part 2: Deposition can take place anywhere between 60° and 160° Fahrenheit. As a general rule, the higher the temperature the better the results, as higher temperatures offer greater ion

Colin Oliver had initially been approached about the charity disc because Teen Cancer Trust knew about Press On Vinyl, and because they knew they were doing small runs with a quick turnaround. By now Press On were also handling orders for established independent labels such as Ninja Tunes, Bella Union and Repertoire, who were all well aware Middlesbrough was the only place they could get their small runs timeously. Colin had just come back from SXSW Festival in Austin. He had made arrangements over there with some of these labels – and been told by a number of people from major labels that they'd been told not to work with Press On because they were renegades and upsetting the apple cart...

Not one to be put off by any of this, Danny told me he was signing the papers the next day for the £180,000 lathe, and that they had even considered having a record shop at the plant.

It was also around now rumours started to circulate that Jack White might be planning a visit to the site to add his support and see how things compared to his Third Man Pressing, which had opened in March 2017. For reference, Third Man's eight custom Newbilt presses were the "first

---

transport rates. But over-temperature can lead to spontaneous plate-out rather the gradual forming required. If insufficient metal ions are present the electrons will be wasted, and plating will not take. The amount of metal deposited, in this case onto the lacquer, is the efficiency of the plating and can approach 100% at low plating rates and high temperatures, but drops off significantly at higher plating rates and lower temperatures. As complicated as all this is it starts to explain how important not just the lacquer itself is, but the impact tiny environmental nuances at any given time can have on the whole process. The deposition is also directly proportional to amperes, so very quickly you have a lot of complicated variables.

significant new influx of machines in probably 35 years, give or take", according to Third Man co-founder Ben Blackwell. The Third Man site's famous Blue Room was, at this time, the only place in the world artists could record live to acetate and almost certainly informed Press On's live-to-lathe concept but the respect was reciprocated as Jack was keen to run his plant along similarly ethical lines as the Middlesbrough plant.

Of course, when I say rumours had started to circulate, I mean Danny had told me it might be on the cards. Whether he did by accident, or as an acknowledgment of the trust we were building, I was under no illusions that if it happened it would be a private visit and not one the local press would be aware of. Gotcha.

The degree of separation was, basically, Colin Oliver had put on the very first White Stripes show in England, so he and Jack go way back. Danny confidently stated: "We'll be meeting up with Jack eventually. He's coming over on tour so I would imagine he'll come then. He wants to set his plant up like ours, but his is more artisan at the moment." (The Jack White tour came and went and, when I mentioned this again later, my question was brushed off – but the very fact Jack White was aware of Press On Vinyl's position on the international stage was something in itself.)

I told Danny the plant was now looking and sounding a lot more like the factory I'd expected. He agreed that everything was a lot more industrious, but said there were still a lot of problems. "You do one run when there's no pressure and it all goes great. Then, when there are loads of people around and [when we are] stepping up to multiple runs, we are finding problems with machines. Skill sets are not quite there yet; knowledge, problem-solving not quite there – but that's the best part: everybody's learning."

However, on this particular day the success of the slow cooker was the only thing on everyone's lips. Danny had seen other people doing splatter-effect vinyl in different ways, and Press On had done it slightly differently again. The main thing was that the finished product played and sounded nice on the turntable in the office. But while the convoluted production process didn't affect the sound quality, it had taken them two and half days to press the run of 500 Low Hummer records. Quite a lot of waste, not just in vinyl, but in running the machines manually and introducing the human element of error.

Danny agreed they wouldn't pressing any more discs that way until they had more machines, and they would have to triple the price to allow for the increased real-time capacity and manpower required to press those types of patterns into the records. He stressed they had gone ahead with the Low Hummer run at the agreed price because they wanted to give it a try, and it was also a chance to run the machines manually for the first time.

He estimated that because that run took so long, it potentially stopped eight other artists getting their records pressed. That was how the company looked at everything – a 50,000 run they had recently been offered would have stopped 100 bands getting a 500-record run. And at that level of the music industry, many of those artists would be reliant on that vinyl to help them raise the finance for their next tour or album: "We would be failing in our mission statement if we went down that route, because it's about getting as many artists their product as possible so they can monetise it and artists can grow and flourish. In the long run, the music industry benefits as well."

Around this time, GZ Vinyl in the Czech Republic had just told their customers they wouldn't be taking any further orders until November, followed by a full year lead time. This was particularly significant as they were traditionally the go-to people for smaller bands and these kinds of developments continued to play into Press On hands. "There definitely isn't anybody doing what we are doing with a focus on that level. I'm not having a go at big labels, but when it was CDs they kicked the arse out of it and the prices were ridiculous when they first came out. Then streaming comes along…"

Ah, the format-less format. For decades within the higher echelons of the music industry, label executives and bosses had fantasised about maximising profits by not having to produce a physical product at all. While not actually being able to conceptualise the product or how it would work pre-internet, when the age of digital recording was ushered in the early 1980s, they were already inadvertently working towards the streaming model of music delivery and consumption. How could they have known it would nearly bankrupt the industry as tech-savvy youngsters quickly learned how to steal the music for free, first via high-profile piracy sites like Napster and later, for those with the know-how, LimeWire and similar?

Apart from YouTube missing a trick at the same time by not introducing a subscription service for what had essentially become a video library for all music ever recorded, the major labels were quick to throw their support behind start-ups like Spotify and the newly above-board Napster to legitimise (and profit hugely from) the new streaming format. The rest is, to coin a phrase, recent history.

Danny was visibly frothing now. "They've ripped the arse out of that now, as well, and only the top artists make money. CDs in the 90s were only 30% of the level they could have been in sound quality. We were told it was a great digital soundscape, but they were using the lowest grade possible just to get them out.[25]

"Man has got a CD press he is trying to bring here for us and it's top grade.[26] He reckons a lot of people will pay top money for that grade of CD, so, again that's just another example of big companies ripping the arse out of culture. They shouldn't be allowed to operate in a culture or arts environment, in my opinion, if that is their aim and if it is going to be to the detriment of the piece of art."

Press On's collective political position is not just for show. Danny, in particular, might stop short of demanding culture be nationalised, there is perhaps something of a cultural revolution bubbling up within him. We talked about Bandcamp joining Epic Games, the Third Man publishing arm's tie-in with Bloomsbury, and Spotify's sponsorship deal with FC Barcelona – all of which had just recently become

---

25 As those of a certain age will remember, early CDs were released with a three-way analogue/digital classification for the recording, mixing and mastering processes with A for analogue and D for digital, respectively. AAD was supposedly the lowest quality, with only the mastering done digitally, and DDD was the highest, with all three parts of the process completed digitally. Some early CD players were also unable to read DDD format, which must have been unbelievably annoying if you had just spent £200 on a player. The Dire Straits album *Brothers In Arms* popularised the DDD format and the classification was soon dropped as nearly all discs were cut this way. Around the same time there was some pushback against CDs from vinyl-loving classical music fans about the sonic frequencies possible on CDs being slightly narrower than on vinyl records, but the results were negligible to even the most fervent of home users.

26 Man's M-Tech company's pioneering Glass CD concept promises to cut the disc direct from laser to glass with practically zero noise reduction and excellent light transmission while an almost perfectly flat surface is easier for CD players to read.

common knowledge. The Third Man info, which Danny was unaware of, seemed to particularly sting, for obvious reasons, but he was on a roll nonetheless…

"None of our directors are money driven. A house in the village and a holiday a year will do for me for the rest of my life. We will always weigh up any opportunities and engage with them, and if it was something we felt we could do, we would – but Bandcamp doing that goes against their independent spirit. It might end up being better, but one thing their users like is that they're an independent company." When the backlash cometh, step up FairSound.

FairSound was now being accelerated for release because of these developments. The success of the Komparrison EP using the FairSound landing page had stoked that fire some more. In fact, it was such a success some additional ultra-limited tour editions of the vinyl were later pressed, with Danny telling me at the time, "We end up with spare PVC that gets mixed up or whatnot, so we'll use some of the mix stuff to make some really funky marble-looking tour-edition vinyl. That's another thing we've got in our favour the way we work with bands."

When I revisited this in June 2022, Elise Harrison (Komparrison singer and Press On Vinyl Customer Account Manager) told me they had five different two-tone marble-effect discs made for the tour which, with the original pink version already sold out, offered fans a second chance to get a limited version of the cut. Although Elise was also quick to clarify they didn't advertise the marble vinyl ahead of time, so as not to detract from sales in independent record stores. The band and fans alike were grateful for the opportunity to get a rare vinyl, and it was another example of Press On going that little bit further.

I guess, if you are the singer in a band, it is always good to have ready access to waste vinyl pellets, as well.

While everything on the surface appeared to be going swimmingly, and from a broader business perspective it was, some minor but persistent pressing problems causing pauses and delays on the factory floor were starting to impact delivery times and with artists having launch shows and release dates approaching, any bad publicity at this juncture would have been a disaster. As ever, though, Press On's devotion to offering the best customer service in the industry prevailed.

The day before my visit, Danny had driven to Manchester to drop off 400 black and 200 green vinyls at Scruff of the Neck Records. It was the first time Press On had done a green run. For context, at this time at the back of the warehouse there was a row of timber yard-style shelving where pallets loaded with metric tonnes of all different coloured pellets were stored, waiting to be used at short notice.

When the test presses for Scruff of the Neck Records came off, the green vinyl had occasional tiny yellow specks in it. The engineers couldn't locate the problem anywhere. They checked the hopper (which feeds the extruder where the pellets are heated to form the puck) and found nothing. But when they checked the sacks of unused pellets, they found that every now and again there was a pellet with a tiny bit of yellow in – just enough to cause a problem with the pressing.

It would have been impossible to sieve out every single offending yellow tainted pellet, so Danny phoned Andy

Gannon from the label. Andy thought it added character, and they were limited edition, anyway. Unsurprisingly, Danny loved that attitude: "In hindsight, I should have just got a handful of yellow pellets and chucked them in so everyone got one."

To put things into context (and this is something that might have happened at many other pressing plants presented with the same scenario): if Press On had sent all the green pellets back it might have added another three months to the lead time while they matched the same green colour. Clearly, not many plants have this level of relationship with the labels they deal with, and Danny explained: "We are keen to be *in* the music industry and understand genres and how labels are run and what can benefit them."

In the relative sanctuary of his office role as director Danny was still planning a concept for 2 June, but now renamed as Independents Day, where they would try to get all the local record shops together. This was inspired by Toni Cook from Bad Neighbour Records, who was doing something similar before Record Store Day but, as ever, Danny wanted to do things bigger — maybe at his beloved Base Camp Boro venue, where he had partied with Opus Kink some months earlier. "We'll get some Press On t-shirts made up with a map of the North East and every independent record shop [marked] on, and try and link them all together…"

It was another event that would not happen, but almost certainly something that might be revisited in future years when finances and/or time allowed. Bad Neighbour Records would, a few months later, relocate to another, larger, venue in Stockton, again leaving Middlesbrough without an independent vinyl stockist while Stockton now had two. Further investigation suggested Stockton's other independent record shop, Sound It Out, were supportive of the move, but it wouldn't take a genius to see a new gap in the Middlesbrough market. Only time would tell how it would be filled…

March also marked one year since Danny and Toddy first got the keys to the Press On building, officially celebrated on 21 March with an inspirational Facebook post about obstacles and mountains. Here's Danny with the origin story of the building itself:

"Got the keys, didn't have any finance in place, we took a massive leap. Me and Toddy had many debates over whether we should do it without the finance in place for a ten-year lease. We weren't going to alter the building at that time so if anything had happened, I don't think they would have held us to an empty building. We were talking to a lot of people and telling things a little differently as to what was going on – not lying, but highlighting certain points, and once we could highlight that we had signed a ten-year lease on a building it sped things up a bit.

"We didn't have the machinery ordered. We didn't start building [inside] until June, and that was just building works and putting the lights in. September to October was a lot of setting up the plant. The galvanics and the plumbing came in November. Without the backend you've got nothing. The gas and water lines. Then, obviously, Christmas Eve…"

However, they were already three months behind where they wanted to be and the two-week shutdown to work on the steam and the mezzanine build would start on 4 April. "Then, from 20 April, it's full steam ahead…" The pun was intentional, I'm sure.

However, for some reason I had an inkling Danny was glossing over things a little and certainly by the end of June, when I finally had a chance to ask Toddy about it (on the pretence of needing to know a bit more technical detail about the state of the plumbing that led to the shutdown), a lot more had happened that would shape the way the business operated in the months to follow...

Toddy: "The first big challenge was how late we got the first two pressing machines, and then the next thing was getting those machines doing anything. When we eventually started pressing, we just started hitting problems straight away due to the design of everything we had done behind the wall with the steam, and we really panicked because we realised we needed a steam accumulator tank and new pipework putting in.

"Once we knew that was the problem the biggest worry was that it would take 16 weeks for an accumulator tank to be built and delivered. Luckily Franco had already been looking into it and managed to get one in six weeks, but we already knew it was going to take two weeks to actually do all the work. The other big worry was whether we were going to have to continue to run for ages knowing one in every five records would have to be discarded before we were able to shut down.

"The temperature of the mould on the pressing machines was fluctuating so much because the pressure wasn't consistent in the boiler. Because of that, the burner time wasn't in sync with the pressing machine. The accumulator tank now means we always have constant pressure, so every single time we press we have the same temperature of the mould. Before, sometimes it was 150° Fahrenheit and sometimes it was 120°. The lower the temperature the more records we had to discard, and it meant we also had to have someone constantly checking that. We couldn't have got going properly and we had already taken quite a few orders because we expected to have been up and running by then. But they are brand new pressing machines in a new country that haven't been tested before."

The two-week shutdown in April put everything back again and also meant that, by then, Press On had taken a number of orders. Luckily, they had been cautious enough not to overstretch themselves too much in these early days, and fortunately had allowed themselves five to six months processing time. However, with the shutdown compounding existing time constraints they suddenly had only six to eight weeks to process the existing orders.

"We weren't even 100% sure the new works were going to work, and we also had to go straight into full production once everything was installed just to not let anyone down."

As luck would have it (because there is something about Toddy and Danny's resolve and determination that makes one suspect they always coming up smelling of roses), they had already made enquiries into getting a lathe.

Originally a cutting room and mastering suite was going to be located elsewhere in Middlesbrough, and Danny had even got as far as looking at a prospective site which they really liked. It meant a lot more money, more rates and more rent for the fledgling company, and it wasn't on the Press On site which had always been a niggling concern.

"Our original plan at the start was to extend the mezzanine deck and have the cutting room and mastering suite there. In the end we didn't, because we were going to have the galvanics underneath it because it had to be near the drains, and it just wasn't logistically possible. In the end the galvanics lab didn't have to be near the drains so we moved it."

So, they ended up going back to the original layout of the plant.

After the decision was made to move the galvanics lab, it was too late to extend the mezzanine deck because of all the dust the build would create – but the forced shutdown handed them a few weeks to get all the materials and enough people to complete the job within the two-week period. No easy task, as they needed the mezzanine deck and front wall that would separate it from the factory floor completing and all the dust clearing away in time for the pressing machines to go back online. Upstairs wouldn't be completely finished, but it was all sealed so they would be able to continue working up there for another two months without disrupting pressing operations back down on the factory floor.

In the end it was the best thing that could have happened. It also gave the guys time to reflect on and sort out a few other issues: "Cash flow is still not amazing; you feel the knock-on effects. We've been playing catch-up for six months now for cash, but it's getting a bit better... But that was definitely the most worrying time."

However, before the shutdown began, another article on Middlesbrough Council's *We Are Middlesbrough* culture website[27] had Danny still talking excitedly about bottling the buzz at the plant into "Middlesbrough distilled" and the hype

---

27   'Being Sound: Going Inside Middlesbrough's First Vinyl Record Plant', Mike Brown, https://www.wearemiddlesbrough.com/our-stories/being-sound-going-inside-middlesbroughs-first-vinyl-record-plant

surrounding the plant at this point was justified, but he was also keen not to keep blaming Adele. "To be fair everything she has done she has released on vinyl."

The article then went on to explain how the project had, understandably taken over their lives, with Toddy being surprisingly honest and terrifyingly understated. "We started out just wanting to get a lathe, then we thought we'd get the next thing, and it snowballed from there."

Day 213

10 May 2022 –

Introducing David Todd

One of the workhorses and tactical brains behind the Press On Vinyl project, we've heard quite a bit from Toddy so far – but who is Managing Director David Todd?

If Danny is the public talisman, then Toddy is the mercurial businessman who glues all the disparate ideas together, discarding those that won't work, and tweaking and aligning those that just might. The Peter Taylor to Danny's Brian Clough, or the Izzy Stradlin to Danny's Slash.

"Ha!"

Toddy might not be as obviously outgoing as Danny, or as full of banter as Tommy and some of the other guys on the factory floor, but he exudes a quiet charisma and self-assurance that ensures he's always in charge. He's the one the others all look to, regardless of the strength of personalities resonating throughout this project. He's the guy that builds rapports and relationships with strangers all over the world online, or over the phone, which means Press On Vinyl is already a global brand to those in the know.

How did it ever get off the ground?

"I was looking at Goosed getting a low-end cutting lathe to cut 20-30 records at a time that we thought might be good for local artists. Around the same time, we had been recording a lot of bands upstairs in Doctor Browns[28] and we wanted to put some of [that music] out as a compilation on vinyl as our first proper release, and so we could sell it and give all the money back to the bands, because that was the ethos of what we were doing at the time. That was September 2019 and everywhere we looked the lead times were about five months, when we wanted it in time for Christmas.

"At that point we didn't know why there were delays, and then we started reading into it. It wasn't as bad as it is now, but it was starting to get that way with capacity, and they were common lead times at all the pressing plants. Goosed was doing mint, we had moved into Sticky Fingers and we were proper buzzing off it. So, we gave up on that one release for Christmas to concentrate on the new location and to build the Goosed brand – but then the pandemic happened, and everything stopped.

"We had been so used to putting all our spare time into something. Then Toni who runs Sticky Fingers was struggling and needed to set up a kitchen to do takeaways. That was

---

28   A longstanding Middlesbrough live music venue that made headlines in 2017 when the then-landlady stated that her punters did not like female rock singers and a social media storm ensued. Now under new ownership with Rock The Foundry's Marc Walsh on board as in-house promoter, normal service has resumed with regular rock and metal nights once more.

going to be next to our studio, which was just going to be ridiculous, trying to record next to a kitchen. The middle floor was going to be a live space, which is now a record shop, so everything was up in the air.

"During that time, me and Danny talked about Press On a lot, getting some research done, getting *obsessed*. We looked at how records are made, why is it so expensive and how it could be made cheaper for smaller artists which, in the end, I found out it can't really. Most importantly, why aren't more people doing it? Because a run of 100 is very expensive when you have to pay for the lacquer and the stamper."

Toddy even looked into HD vinyl (where it's not necessary to cut a lacquer, and the stamper is made straight from a laser). It turned out the technology was still at the research stage and it would mainly be used for long runs, as the stamper won't need replacing. So it would be cheaper the more records can be pressed. Toddy had to admit he was barking up the wrong tree, so he tried another tree…

"…and fan-funded campaigns, because if you can't make it cheaper how can you make it easier to raise funds? And that's when we started thinking about FairSound… That was my train of thought, and I was bouncing stuff off Danny and talking on the phone for hours every night…"

As our chat was interrupted by a minor issue from the factory floor, it occurred to me how approachable Toddy is to all the other staff. Having worked in offices for 20-odd years, I've never known a director of a company so hands-on that the staff feel comfortable enough to break up a meeting with "Yo, Todd…" That in itself is a credit to the company structure they had built.

"I'd worked at Tees Foyboatmen since I was 18. My dad worked there, my uncle worked there, my step-brother still works there, my grandad worked there. I wouldn't say it's a family business, but there were lots of families there... My grandad started it with about six other people with some boats on the river, and they used to go out to meet ships and ask if they needed a mooring service then basically get the ropes out for it. Eventually, when it got busy, the port said they would need to all work together and make a company. That was 60 years ago, and I did that as well until a year ago."

That stretch of the River Tees after the end of the war would have been a bustling mini-metropolis of trades and markets populated by businessmen, chancers and ne'er do wells, an almost Dickensian scene as suburban Middlesbrough thrived and expanded at speed while the old town remained resolutely working class and as rough as an uncut diamond.

Now in his mid-30s, Toddy is outwardly relaxed and cool. A family man, his wife Kerry also works at the plant, and a nephew would do work experience there in July, mirroring the small acorn Tees Foyboatmen must have grown from.

"Once we'd done five years [as foyboatmen] we all got an equal share in the company," that socialist mentality instilled early, "so I wouldn't say I have a business background, but I'd been on the board for four years, so I had a rough idea. The first thing that happened when I told Danny about [the pressing plant idea] is that normally I go down a rabbit hole and then forget about it, but Danny was persistent that we had to do it and he wouldn't let me leave it. He knew about this place being empty, and some people we should speak to at Tees Valley Business Association (TVBA), John Leer and James Latcham. We had a meeting with them, and I said to Danny, 'Don't you think we will need a business plan?' But he thought they would just love it!"

At this point neither Danny nor Toddy had done any costings, other than knowing it was going to cost a lot. What Toddy did know, even at this early stage, was that they weren't going to be able to proceed with Press On Vinyl on a small scale with just one press: "You have to go full out. I knew how much the presses cost and I had a rough idea how much the steam and cooling might cost, and I knew it was in the hundreds of thousands of pounds." Naturally he also wondered how they would persuade people to back them with nothing but an idea as, at that stage, the pair didn't have any spare cash.

They had the meeting with John and James who did, indeed, love it. They advised them what grants were available based on the number of jobs they could potentially create and the benefits to the local area based on capital expenditure. "The way it works is, you don't get the cash up front. You apply for the grant, but then you get the money when you've actually spent it. You have to prove you are hiring people and spending what you said you would spend, and you get that much of your grant back each quarter ratioed." However, the first grant legitimised the company and proved due diligence. John and James also put Danny and Toddy in touch with people who helped them secure private and debt funding, which was the next stage.

Then, as you would expect, John asked Toddy if he had a business plan and Toddy told him, sure, he was just finishing it off, before immediately going home and Googling how to write a business plan. "The beauty of it was, I downloaded a template, and this is how I really knew it was a good idea: every single thing I knew how to answer (apart from the financials which took ages)... We handed it in two weeks later and they thought it was class."

With the grant secured, the largest TVBA had awarded for a start-up company (although technically they still had no money because of the way it was to be allocated), they spoke to David Hynes, who had backed them from the beginning. He promised to invest financially, eventually becoming a fellow director as a result. "Me and Danny didn't even put ourselves on the books until quite far in, so Danny was still working for David and I was still on the foyboats. There were other people on the books here before we quit our other jobs."

Family and friends were also quick, then, to offer support where they could. Some put money in, but the fledgling business were still short of their initial target amount so had to start looking into securing some debt finance.

Although finance companies the pair approached were often impressed with the Press On Vinyl business plan, the country was now in the middle of a pandemic and obliged to give out interim seagull loans as part of the government's fiscal response, so they couldn't justify that type of finance at that time. Then a financier who had originally turned them down, FW Capital, got back in touch.

FW Capital look after Northern Powerhouse money and link their debt risk to job creation too. Having immediately seen it was good for the local area, and with a more stable outlook post-lockdowns, it got back in touch and it was, again, down to Toddy to sell the Press On Vinyl vision. "It took a lot to prove that there was a market out there. The same crack about having a load of records in the loft," Toddy would later simplify the conversation, with the benefit of having already secured the money.

Fifteen years ago, there were far fewer pressing plants, but there were only certain labels releasing vinyl, which meant lead times were often less than a month. Plants were looking for work and the presses weren't at full capacity. Even as recently as four to five years ago the lead time at most plants was three to four months, which is what Press On Vinyl offer now. Any longer than that feels too lengthy when small and new acts often release something new every few months.

With some plants now offering 12-month lead times, or not even taking orders, it is easy to see how things have got out of hand. But for many people with nothing more than a vague interest in digging out that old turntable and buying a Rumours repress, it was still not a very visible problem to those outside of the vinyl community.

I asked Toddy about that time, when they were trying to secure the finance for the company. Even the pacing of his answers made me a little anxious about whether they could, even now, still bring it all home.

"We had the grant, but it wasn't equivalent to any money; we had a nice chunk from family and friends and David [Hynes]. We had [the offer of a] loan, but dependant on a final piece of private finance to back it up, [and it] only had a three-month lifespan... so, we did a couple of pitch events on Zoom during the pandemic.

The first one Danny did the talking and I answered the questions. I was too nervous to do the presentation. We had a meeting prior with North Invest, who talked us through the business plan and how to write a pitch and Danny delivered it. Then on the second one he was stuck at work and I'd been up all night at my job. I nearly turned the Zoom off and was going to say to Danny we got nothing. I made myself do it and I thought it was terrible, but it just so happened Colin [Oliver] had been invited to it because one of the accountants who were putting the event on partnered with North Invest worked for Colin and thought he would like [our pitch]."

The similarities with Alan McGee discovering Oasis at King Tuts Wah Wah Hut after only having been persuaded to go out at the last minute will not be lost on many. Apparently Colin was similarly impressed, later admitting he was listening to all those pitches and was about to turn off, but in the end Toddy got talking. He finally invested in Press On Vinyl the day that the loan offer was going to run out.

"So, in the middle of all that we had to sign the lease as well, because someone else was looking at the building. So, we didn't have all the finance in place, but it was looking pretty good…"

Today it's impossible to visit TeesAMP without being drawn to Press On Vinyl's plot with its distinctive colour scheme around the glass front of the office, but a similar aesthetic permeates the whole park, if not always as obviously. It's not your normal industrial estate; it's got a quirkiness to it.

"We came into it not really manufacturers, as such, but we had enough about us to know we would either know people or we'd learn ourselves, 'cause that's what Danny's like. Quite a lot of people working here now are engineers or maintenance people. A lot of people out there doing the more responsible roles have taken wage cuts to learn something new."

Toddy's use of the collective 'we' in everything he talks about is definitely worth noting, especially when he talks about things I already knew from Danny had been all Toddy's work. Danny would pull me up later for not using the same pronoun.

A common thread in our chats around this time was how important working with Franco and Man from the outset had been, and the priceless consultancy they brought with them. There was also the North American consultant, who I was allowed to know had been on site for about three weeks in January before a planned return in June. His backstory is: he started off at a printing company as a broker before eventually investing in some vinyl presses. When that novelty wore off, he set up as a consultant and worked for years with certain plants helping them set up. Like a background Simpsons character, it seems there might always be more to them, but we'll leave him there, tantalisingly mysterious. Perhaps they carved him from a bigger spoon.

On a serious note, given that some of this consultancy sounded pretty expensive, I decided this might be time to ask how much had already been spent on the Press On Vinyl project and Toddy was surprisingly forthright. "With the loans, the first bit of investment and the grant it's about £1.2m but we've injected more money since, so probably about £1.5m not including the lathe and all the extra stuff. By the end of the year [2022] it will be about £2m. It seemed ridiculous at first, because I've never dealt with figures like that before, but it's all relative isn't it? The loan and grant companies do all the due diligence, so the business plan has to be iron-tight, and they know that some won't work out and some will.

"At the moment it's very stressful, because the first few orders that we are trying to get out on time are either behind because of the shutdown, or the printers have been behind due to COVID. Sometimes we've been ready to do stuff and we haven't had the labels, so it's constant firefighting and putting plasters over stuff. We have a great day where everything is on target and then the next day you get hardly anything done, and it's that frustration of the up and down. But once we get over these first few orders, most of which should be out on time this week, it should settle down. People have been driving all over the country dropping stuff off on the day they were due."

It was only about six weeks later, in June, when I spoke to Danny again, that I realised the significance of what Toddy had told me: the truth was, production nearly stopped entirely and they would have had to consider refunds. Even later, Danny would admit it nearly set a completely different course for the company, if not quite at risk of bankrupting them…

Danny also told me Toddy had been to London on the Monday that week, someone else went to Norwich on Tuesday and so on. There was a delivery needed for an event in Glasgow on the Saturday where the records had been pressed but the sleeves hadn't arrived. COVID still hung heavy in the air, quite literally in some places. Not to be deterred, as we know by now, Toddy decided to put 30 of the run into disco sleeves (anti-static paper sleeves with a clear centre) free of charge and drop them off himself.

Toddy: "I was going to Glasgow anyway to watch Komparrison, so I dropped [the discs] off so they had some with the disco sleeves to sell at the launch event, and then we delivered the rest a couple of days late. So, it's thinking of ways to go that extra mile. We use a few different printers and the quality is always good but the turnaround [time] has been double or quadruple sometimes, which is not always really their fault. Everyone was getting stuff online during lockdown and delivery boxes use a similar pulp to the sleeves we use, so there is a shortage of card now as well."

By all accounts, Tommy loves proofing the artwork, and for the team it was almost as exciting seeing the sleeves of the first few they got back as it was to see the records themselves. When those first orders had started coming back from the printers in late 2021, the only worry any of the team had had was waiting for the machines to arrive.

Danny: "Man and Franco are great guys but at the end of the day we sent them loads of money and we didn't really know how good the machines were going to be, if and when they would arrive. Franco comes back and forth now from Italy, he's not here at the moment. Man went back to Hong Kong yesterday, but he's been here since the end of November. He's going back to his factory in China to sort some stuff out then moving his family here in August. By then we'll have our next two or three machines arriving, so he'll come and sort them, but we are also talking about working quite closely with him for more presses in another plant. Us, him and Franco should be working quite closely together for the next couple of years at least..."

While the general spirit of the company thrived off a certain amount of hyperbole, I wondered: realistically, what might happen over the next year or so?

"We need to get more baths in the galvanics lab so we have more capacity there. We could look at building another lab but it's also having to train people up. There are only some people can hack doing [the galvanics] all the time because it's quite claustrophobic and there are so many variables that even the slightest mistake can damage the lacquer. You have to care enough to not make too many mistakes, but when you do to not take it to heart. We've got some really good people in there now but to think we would build a massive department, it's difficult.

"Priority at the moment is to get a few more people trained up in there with a couple of extra baths so we can run 24 hours alongside the two additional presses. Then the cutting studio. They are the main plans for this year. Possibly three machines coming in the summer, might end up with a sixth one. We've got the cooling system for six so the sixth might just run test presses and all the cool arty stuff that takes ages to do."

This was Toddy at his most passionate and most loyal to the Press On ethos. To think an extra machine would be dedicated purely to artist frivolity and experimenting will sound to many in the business as financial folly but to Toddy it was just the way it should be. Artist integrity above all and in its purest form possible.

While previously Danny and Toddy had discussed the new presses arriving in parts to be assembled on site, they for now they will arrive ready built. "There is potential when Man moves [permanently to the UK], and if we get another plant, we might build them here, but these are just conversations at the moment and we don't know how it's going to pan out. We've got some of the bigger labels in the UK asking for capacity, and they get that our ethos is not doing huge runs and we aren't going to give half capacity away to one big label."

Contrary to some negative chatter, Press On had never said they *wouldn't* work with the big labels, only that it was a matter of capacity. True to that ethos was that they would talk to anybody before making final decisions so, while one of the labels Toddy talks of distributes two million records a year and another has 10% of all UK vinyl going through their distribution network, neither are affiliated to any of the big four major labels. The latter being invited for a visit.

"They are coming up to see the place and they've given us one little run to do as a test. They've asked us to do the smaller runs and some of the limited edition runs that go with the big runs, and we would be doing them a big favour. We just wouldn't do the big runs. They get that and respect that. These guys have capacity at the big plants still, but if we fit into their schedule and it's a small run then that's fine for everyone."

In fact, word was this particular label had tried to set up a plant in 2019. It had had the finance in place, or at least readily available, but had discovered the real difficulty is finding the right people to run the plant. It would have had to pull people out of their existing jobs at the label or in the retail sector, which then potentially leads to loss of revenue in those areas of the business. The label was subsequently looking for plants where it could buy a machine and have the plant run it, similar to the barber-stool method where barbers rent a chair in existing barber shops. While this is something Press On Vinyl had decided they would never do, it is an option open to them within the industry, in terms of guaranteeing certain capacity through a contractual arrangement. It's suddenly obvious why other plants snap up these opportunities.

"We wouldn't do that here because I strongly believe five machines is enough for us to do everything we are planning with smaller labels. But we are part of the industry as well now, so to think that we would never do anything for the industry itself is not looking at the bigger picture. So, we are now discussing how we can build a second plant so that it doesn't affect what we are doing here, but it does provide capacity for bigger labels and will allow us to move some of the expertise from here and add more.

"The other problem is access to machines – but with Man and Franco we have got access to machines at a rate of two or three per year. A year from now we probably will have enough staff to start training more somewhere else and they [the big labels] have got some cash to help fund that." Admittedly this wasn't something I expected Toddy to talk openly about, but it did address how far things had come and how fast things continued to move for them. "It definitely doesn't affect the ethos of what we are trying to do here, and it is helping the industry. The hardest thing is training people up, basically. That's our future. It *might* happen, but you have to start looking into it now."

As we've seen with the case studies mentioned earlier, some of the bigger plants in the world are also expanding to try and soak up demand, so Press On's access to a steady trickle of machines puts them in a very sound position. However, there will certainly be a time in the next few years when capacity at other presses becomes less of an issue. Toddy had already considered that:

"[It's] why we've done it now… if we get it right and show we are easier to work with, communicate with, go that extra mile and quality is good, there is no reason why anyone would move away. Hopefully we can do it with these labels before there is loads of capacity worldwide and they don't think it's worth it. Everything is timing, and we timed the first bit perfectly, so now if we want to go ahead with the second part, we need to get on with it soon.

"People love to help though, I've spoken to loads of people on the phone getting advice and help, so if I don't talk to other people as well I think that is a bit wrong. I imagine there are some people in some plants that wouldn't want to talk to you, but everyone I've spoken to has been nothing but helpful. Stamper Discs[29], who we were going to work with and then didn't, have given us loads of help and they get nothing out of it. We have bought a few stampers off them recently but nothing major. In fact, they really just did that to help out because we had an emergency. And in the future they might have an issue and we can help them, or staff swapping, if either of us have a member of staff off sick for a few weeks, for example."

---

29 Stamper Discs is a Sheffield-based company specialising in electroforming in the vinyl industry. It's run by Martin Frings, who spent three years learning his craft at The Vinyl Factory in London, before setting up Stamper Discs in 2018. He's also operated EMI, Toolex and Viryl presses at different plants. Press On Vinyl originally intended to use the company for all their stampers before Franco persuaded them to build their galvanics lab on site.

By late spring, FairSound had become something of a minor thorn in Press On Vinyl's side. Progress was slow on the website build, but Danny and Toddy were struggling to find the time and the energy to put into it. It was perhaps the first sign that the Press On wheels were in danger of wobbling, if not falling off. This sudden lack of motivation caused a major rethink.

The whole idea with FairSound was for it to offer a more affordable and achievable platform for independent artists, with on-site crowdfunding being the main attraction. Originally imagined as part of the Press On Vinyl website, it had its own website before snowballing into a multi-media marketplace with venues, a record shop and a social network.

Toddy would sometimes slip into matter-of-factness, but was perhaps even despondent at how FairSound had progressed. "We were shown the almost finished product, and it is really messy and clunky. We don't really like what we've seen with everything battling against each other. The social network aspect was initially the least of our priorities, but the company we got to build it specialises in that. For them, you can't build the other stuff without that being the main thing and there are all the issues of running a community online. Policing it, content, moderating it… when the main part for us was just to help artists fund vinyl releases. Now we don't know whether we will do FairSound.com or whether we will do it all on Press On Vinyl because, at the end of the day, we have built Press On Vinyl as a brand already and people are talking about it, so to then introduce a second brand could get a bit messy."

So, they decided, after a couple of weeks of stressful toing and froing, to ditch the community side completely to concentrate on getting the original concept over the line, do it well and then slowly introduce the other parts.

In hindsight, FairSound always seemed like a big ask for a brand-new company alongside the pressing plant and in the competitive world of social media – social media being what it always looked like it would become, from the outside. Similarly, logic suggests that the ideal time to introduce a second brand would be at such a time the first brand was generally regarded as a success or perhaps at the peak of its PR curve, not while it was still on the upward slope.

"We're not ditching the name FairSound, it might be a sub-domain, or it might be a campaign name or a by-line. At the end of the day we've got a lot of the development done, so it's definitely going on Press On Vinyl somewhere."

"There is a logic to every single thing we've done but you sometimes have to go back over and reassess. We're all quite good at not being too hung up on our own ideas. In the back of my mind it was niggling that we were doing too much with FairSound and it was not going to work. But in a couple of months there will be a platform of some kind for artists to fund a record, which will be perfect timing because we will have the new presses. If we have an influx of orders we will be able to support it, and if it is a slow burner we will just go back to some more labels to fill capacity that way and monitor it as it grows."

I asked Toddy again where he thought Press On was likely to be by October given this bump in the road. He reverted to Company Director mode. "The new machines will be here in July or August; we'll definitely have the lathe, maybe even recording in the plant; definitely have done a performance in the downstairs room; and definitely have some sort of funding platform up and running and it be common knowledge; and almost up to capacity in the plant."

I also asked about 7" capacity, as that was something often mentioned as an affordable first step for new artists. "We just need to buy a mould and a few bits of adaptors for the forming equipment, but we just haven't had the cash to do it yet. By the end of the year, we will be doing 7"s. We never intended to do it before we get the next three machines. Then we need to order the mould, which takes three months, and we are not in a position to buy it now as cash is proper tight."

By the beginning of May, with the two-week shutdown completed in two-and-half weeks, the inside of the Press On Vinyl compound was looking very different, with a ground-floor live music area boxed off, and a lathe room and mastering suite under construction immediately above, all to be fully soundproofed to avoid any noise pollution in the mastering suite and free from vibration issues on the plant floor. Toddy had already explained how this was the next stage of the Press On vision of doing as much as possible on site.

On 12 May, a wonderfully creative interview with Colin Young from *North East Times Magazine*[30] introduced the live-to-lathe concept to the world, or at least those reading local independent media.

Toddy told me they had nearly signed a lease somewhere else for a studio to house the lathe. But then he showed me a basic wood-panelled room on the ground floor near the presses, where nothing had been so far, and I began to see his vision being realised.

"This is going to be the live room; we're going to soundproof it and full bands can play here and we will record

---

30 'Leading The Vinyl Revival', Pete Mallon, 12 May 2022, https://netimesmagazine.co.uk/promoted/leading-the-vinyl-revival/

it straight to the lathe, which will be upstairs. That will be a big window over there so they can look out over the plant as they record."

Upstairs, in the newly constructed mezzanine complex of rooms, specifically the cutting room, Toddy explained how they wouldn't be able to use it all the time. Making the masters and cutting on the lathe takes time, and the lathe would also be needed for all their other orders. But he was sure they could make the concept work. "Even if we only do it four or five times a year and get certain bands in, we could make a film about it. We are the only people in the world doing it, definitely nobody else in a pressing plant. Then we will mix it in the mastering suite next door, on the fly, and then cut it on the fly too, so if anyone makes a mistake in the studio or cutting it, we'll have to start again."

Given the layout of the plant and the space at their disposal beyond the constraints of the plumbing and pressing set-up, it was certainly a no-brainer to have everything on site if possible. Danny later let slip that a band were pencilled in for 21 December, to test out the live room. Given his contacts at the time I guessed it would be Opus Kink but, as we have seen, things often move at speed with Press On Vinyl.

We were now in what would become the mastering suite, a similar wood-lined box room, unfinished, with the layered wall cavities still visible in places that would eventually ensure state-of-the-art soundproofing, essentially two 'floating' rooms independent from the rest of the plant. "It doesn't go through any computers or anything, and is the most analogue sound you can get because it's just going straight to the vinyl. Set up, if they can do it in one take, then you've got the master disc, walk it downstairs, two hours to make the stamper and then however long it takes to press.

In theory, if we order all the printed parts in advance, you could have a mint video of a full day seeing them set up and rehearsing, and then cutting and pressing it. Whether it's us doing it or a label asking us to do it for them, they could sell them for a fortune."

Toddy said it was always something they wanted to do, one of his and Danny's first ideas, in fact. Perhaps rightly, they had reined it in a bit, but now, with a lot more confidence in the business and its finances they were pushing forward again with the original plan. The lathe became available and they felt they had to go for it. With Alex Balzama from Swift Mastering as Head of Audio, Mastering and Lacquer Cutting, time would almost certainly tell that this was another inspired decision.

Alex is a classically trained musician and producer. He set up Swift Mastering in Battersea in 2008, but since 2018 has been working on separating the mixing and mastering processes so Battersea could be refurbished into a fully-fledged production house. This will allow Alex to relocate his young family to North Yorkshire where his online mastering operation will be located solely at Press On Vinyl. "Eighty percent of cutting is mastering, and he's been doing it for 30 years, so he's going to train Papa Goose [Nigel Crooks, Pressing Operator and former Chief Sound Engineer, School of Arts and Media at Teesside University] on the cutting as he's already mastering in here as well."

Later, after the lathe had been received but was still under lock and key, Danny told me they would be working with Crispin Murray who would commission the lathe for use and has experience of live-to-lathe recording. Pete Norman at Finyl Tweek would also advise, and was due on site in late September. Mastering Engineer Lewis Hopkins at

Stardelta Audio Mastering[31] would also analyse everything they produced and would come to have a more prominent, if understated, role to play in the development of this particular project we will hear more about later.

As we know, the three main processes are the cutting, stamping and pressing, so the lathe was the final piece of that production line. Having previously been advised to only do the pressing on site, it was Franco who said the team needed to do the stamping as well because if something went wrong at that stage it would create delays waiting for a replacement stamper. With the current backlogs in stamper production, it was a good job they did.

Of the cutting itself, it's a similar scenario to the galvanics and the pressing machines in that it is often very hard to get anyone that has either done it before or is really good at mastering. Added to that, a good quality lathe may only be available once a year. Lathes haven't really been made since the 1980s. The VMS80 Press On were getting was pretty much the best available and the last one Neumann[32] ever made so, ergo, not many left in the world. It later transpired this particular lathe was owned by a legendary drum and bass producer who, for one reason or another, wanted to offload his stock.

---

31   Stardelta Audio Mastering is a state-of-the-art mastering facility located deep in Dartmoor National Park in Devon. It aims to make real analogue mastering accessible to all by using a combination of the finest analogue and digital equipment available.
32   Berlin-based Neumann were the only company to offer the full record-cutting system: the lathe, cutter head and electronics. The VMS80 is the same model that they use at Abbey Road Studios, which is an updated version of the VMS66 and VMS70. It's still the go-to model for many. The only other brands of record-cutting lathes still in operation are Scully in Connecticut and Lyrec of Copenhagen.

Toddy: "If we didn't have the stampers there would be a 16-week delay waiting for them and then, if anything goes wrong, further delays… At the minute, the cutting isn't too bad in the UK as there are a couple of studios that can turn it round quite quickly, but it will affect that eventually because all the plants are trying to do more, and then there will be a shortage of lacquers. On top of all that, [having a lathe] just makes things run smoother. We can get the audio and then our guys look after it all, so if we mess up a stamper we don't have to order another lacquer which costs £250 a time as well. If we scratch a stamper, we can do another the next day."

The lathe cuts the lacquer in real time, but the first time it's done, it's not always mastered perfectly so then Alex will go back into the studio and either reject it or do a little bit more mastering. The cutting is an extremely important part of the whole process, perhaps *the* most important part.

When the guys first do a test press they mainly listen to the lacquer cut, how it translates to the stamper and how it is pressing, but they are also looking for other issues. For example, if there is a lot of distortion on the masters, you might lose the high end, or it might be because it hasn't been cut or mastered properly. If there is crackling, it might be because it wasn't silvered properly; surface noise might be because it wasn't pressed properly. The majority of problems a trained eye would be able to see by looking, but any problems with the cutting and stampers you can hear. That is what the test presses are for.

With everything else not only in-house but on-site, it made sense to me that the printing aspect might also be brought under the same roof, but for Toddy, it seemed, this was a bridge too far at this stage.

"We might get a digital printer for short runs of 300 to 400, but to do long runs or gatefolds we would need an industrial thermal printer. They cost a fortune and take up loads of space so we would need to do other printing work to justify the outlay. Never say never, but if we did it probably wouldn't be in this building because of space." This had become a common theme now, thinking outside of the box or, literally, thinking outside of the building for other ventures, whether a printing press or a recording studio. It was telling of how confident Toddy was in the company's success and profitability.

In what would become the mastering suite:

"You have to calculate all the distances and ratios and heights because it affects the sound inside." Showing me an intricate-looking piece of joinery at floor level Toddy explained, "This level here will be isolated from the floor, and then the studio floor will be isolated from that, to be as close to 100% soundproof as possible. It's noisy down there in the plant, so you need a nice quiet space to listen back and we can't have any vibrations going back through the other way either because it might make the needle on the lathe jump. Air gaps help with soundproofing. The band room downstairs will be all wired up into here so we can mix it straight down into two tracks, a left and a right, and that will be fed straight into the cutting room when we are doing live-to-lathe."

Ironically, before magnetic tape became widely available in 1948, masters were always cut live to disc, so the live-to-lathe concept is something of a full-circle return to a more authentic analogue process that would appeal to the team whether they realise it or not – although Toddy's enthusiasm for all things analogue perhaps suggests they do. In fact, Toddy's dad is a keen vinyl collector of some renown.

Back on the floor, the plant was now operating two eight-hour shifts from 6am to 10pm, seven days a week, but not without some ongoing processing issues.

However, following on from the success of the Komparrison EP and the limited tour edition, a further unique marbled version of the release was made, to showcase the flexibility of the coloured and unusual vinyl Press On were offering. It was available exclusively to Sound It Out records in Stockton, to coincide with Record Store Day 2022 on 23 April. It promptly sold out on the day.

Coincidentally, around this time, CD Unity also started popping up on my Facebook feed offering 16-week turnaround on vinyl. It appeared to be in direct response to Press On, so let's take a closer look.

The Edinburgh-based company was formed in 2017 with the aim of, as the name suggests, providing incredible-looking CDs at affordable prices. Their website promotes an eco-friendly approach and they have built a loyal clientele, including corporate and independent artists, where each client benefits from individual attention from the company's dedicated team of graphic designers and audio engineers. If the ethos sounds familiar, that's because it is.

On closer inspection, CD Unity is part of Audio Unity Group, which appears to be a collective of engineers and musicians providing high-end audio solutions. All very admirable. As far as CD Unity's vinyl operation is concerned, they offer the standard pressing, test pressing and artwork proofing, as well as a choice of coloured vinyl, 140g or 180g,

12" or 7". Their usual lead time is nine months but, crucially, now they are offering express slots of 16 weeks, presumably at a premium.

CD Unity's 12" Single Sleeve Vinyl package includes master cut and galvanics for both sides, full-colour labels, white inner sleeves, outer sleeves printed on 300g card stock, full colour A/B labels, five test presses, assembly and boxing, UK delivery and mastering.

The main takeaways here are perhaps the importance of the galvanics and mastering aspect on quick turnarounds, something Press On were right to secure early on in the company's development. Secondly, the difference in approach to the magic 16-week number. One suspects CD Unity has some other tie-ins elsewhere preventing them from offering 16-week as standard.

Staying true to Press On ethics, the company hastily arranged a Ukrainian fundraiser to take place on the Queen's Jubilee weekend (1 June) – before being just as quickly cancelled because the Ukrainian band Love'n'Joy, who had already completed a number of dates across the EU, were denied a British visa.

All the while, names like Charlie Simpson and, somewhat unbelievably, Michael Jackson were coming, literally, hot off the presses. At this time, Toddy also mentioned "something big" that might be happening in the next few weeks. He would only cryptically tell me it might alter the following chapters of the book, and that I should prepare myself for an unscheduled visit at short notice. However, as the Jubilee passed, and I immersed myself in my day job and a flurry of family commitments, I heard little from Toddy and the boys other than the occasional WhatsApp message or exclusive look at some photos before they were published on Press On social media.

Photographs ©Kerry Todd

Photographs ©Kerry Todd

Photographs ©Kerry Todd

RIP Nigel Crooks (Papa Goose)

Photographs ©Kerry Todd

Introducing
Colin Oliver

Entrepreneur and Futuresound founder Colin Oliver is a very self-assured man, and why shouldn't he be? Director of 12 successful companies, all with links to each other, as well as Futuresound, itself a multi-million-pound endeavour with links to many medium- to large-scale music events across Yorkshire. When we finally caught up for a chat, he was not what I was expecting. Smart casual dress, in desert boots, Levi's jeans and an expensive-looking overshirt, and *very* easy to chat to. Not at all the slightly imposing besuited businessman I had envisioned.

It would also be easy to assume Colin would be the voice of reason to Danny and Toddy's exuberant ideas machine, but if anything Colin's commitment to the Press On ethos at least matched anything I'd already seen at the plant.

The company's fourth director, David Hynes, on the other hand, is a little harder to read and, indeed, pin down. Expensively dressed on the one occasion we are briefly introduced, he has the youthful demeanour and confidence the director of a successful alarm-fitting company (with the Teesside Airport contract, amongst others) can afford. Press On Vinyl appears to be his first formal financial venture away from his day job. However, a number of emails and nudges later, he proved just aloof enough to avoid interrogation here, whether by intention or schedule.

However, I did manage to talk to Colin on one of his visits to the plant where he was trying to conduct a flurry of in-person meetings, while downstairs the first, subsequently aborted, attempt to press a record made of sugar starch was going on. He was typically unflappable, only quipping that he hoped my questions weren't too personal, by way of a passive-aggressive icebreaker.

Colin's Press On story in a nutshell is that his accountant already knew that ten years ago he had tried to set up a pressing plant, even getting as far as buying a couple of pressing machines from the Czech Republic before realising, as many had done before him, that he didn't have anyone to set up the plant and do the manufacturing. So, the idea was eventually shelved, if not completely dispensed with. Then Colin's accountant told him that Toddy, Danny and David Hynes were looking at setting up a vinyl pressing plant.

Colin talks in a captivating Southern drawl; he was born in Dorset but has lived in Yorkshire for over 30 years:

"I had to go on one of those online pitches and, unfortunately for me, Toddy was the last person on, so I just muted it, made a cup of tea and waited for his turn to talk. Within about 20 minutes of his pitch I was already bought in. It was the missing link for me. They were getting the keys shortly after so I agreed to invest, but I knew straight away it was more than just investment because it's something I'm passionate about and I wanted to get indie bands and small labels to the front of the queue."

Even at that stage, it was the ethos that attracted Colin to the venture more than financial gain, but he explained that it was more recent Press On initiatives such as the recording studio that really interested him, things that Toddy and Danny were already talking about early doors.

Of Colin's own pressing plant plans, he told me it had been "more of a Hit Factory[33] approach really, because we had the studio downstairs in the property I've got in Leeds (Munro House[34]) with a rehearsal room in the basement, and that is where we were going to put our pressing plant originally. It was not on the same scale as this – it was only ever going to be two machines – but looking back and knowing what I know now here it would probably have been a nightmare!

"Unless you have the contacts that [Danny and Toddy] have made with Franco, Man and the others, it would be impossible. Doing the galvanics first makes total sense now. It wasn't supposed to be like that, but the machines were delayed and delayed and that was the only thing we could work on." While this account of the late 2021 activity at the

---

33   New York recording studio founded in 1969 but made famous by the likes of Hall & Oates, Peter Gabriel and Paul Simon in the 1980s and latterly Mark Ronson and Kanye West.

34   Situated on the corner of Duke Street and York Street, Munro House is an iconic art-deco build in the centre of Leeds in an area now known as modern Leeds's cultural centre and officially known as the Arts Quarter. It also houses an artisan bakery.

plant might differ slightly from Danny and Toddy's, it sheds some valuable light on those dark months before the first two pressing machines arrived. "...but it turned out to be the right thing. That side of the business is always going to be temperamental but doing it now and getting it right has been the essence really.

"Part of the reason I bought into Press On was Danny, Toddy and David's vison and attitude." It was unusual to hear Colin mention David Hynes so much. I had come to think of him more as a silent partner, but his involvement is clearly more with Colin on the business side than the manufacturing side. "The relationships they've built [with external businesses], it certainly wasn't like that at the start but everyone who works here has got the same goal and understanding."

By the time Toddy and Danny got the keys to the plant, Colin had already committed and sorted out the financial and logistic side of things at his end. But he was still very much in the dark, having not even visited the Press On Vinyl site yet. "They were getting excited about a big shed in the middle of nowhere, and I don't know what I was expecting but I came up and as soon as I drove into Teesside, I had this feeling... It's no secret that Middlesbrough and Teesside have been kicked around the dancefloor with the highs and then the lows of industry, but having seen the building empty I drove back to Leeds laughing my head off at what they were going to do with it. Then when I came up the second time, they had just started to paint everything yellow. I'd been to Third Man in Detroit, and that's all yellow, and I thought it was to do with that. So, I told Danny to go the council and find out what colour the Transporter Bridge is and that's what we should be concentrating on, finding our own identity."

Presumably that was when Tommy hot-footed it down to the bridge himself to scrape a flake off to take to B&Q.

The elephant in the room here, again, is that ill-advised 60-day countdown way-back-when, when Danny and Toddy first picked up the keys. Colin wasn't one for shirking the question. "Marketing is great at getting to local people, but I've never been one for shouting about what I do, far from it, I'm very much get on and people will come. They are all very proud Boro boys here, but they couldn't see the wood for the trees at times and it was good for them to hear [what a great thing they have here] and not just someone else telling them to move down to Leeds.

"The early marketing reached out too far, and all of a sudden people were knocking on the door before we were even ready. That could have been detrimental to the business. It's only been the last couple of months that we have been at full capacity and now the focus has gone onto FairSound. Once we've done all the marketing and PR for that, then we can pull the marketing department back onto Press On and then, when we've got four machines, we can have another little shout again and this time we'll be open for business."

This was something Harry Ridgway from Hanglands agreed with. He told me. "We didn't actually wipe anything [off the socials] but I think once we had sent the PR out and raised with the team that the socials might need a bit of care and attention, the early 60-day countdown had long been abandoned.

"My initial thoughts were that it sounded great, and when I drove up to Teesside to meet everyone, upon arriving I was greeted with this amazing group of passionate people working on something they loved with a deeply principled and serious understanding amongst all the excitement.

Myself and Sam (Airey, also of Hanglands) were talking in the car on the way home and just decided we needed to be a part of it as much as possible..."

"The PR was interesting as what we initially expected would be a fairly industry story landed at a time when the vinyl crisis and pressing delays were being discussed in the news. There was a narrative around major labels gobbling up capacity and specific artists being responsible for vinyl delays, so this additional news story that there was a UK vinyl plant opening, and one that would service the independent music industry, really caught people's imagination.

"Again, to their massive credit, the team responded brilliantly to a huge amount of media interest and really just wanted to talk to everyone about what they were doing. I don't think we expected to be booking David Todd onto Front Row on Radio 4, but he did brilliantly. I feel strongly that you can't fake authenticity and the passion and knowledge on display here meant we could put them up for basically everything and they'd do alright..."

Colin: "For me, I've got 12 different businesses, but they are all interlinked. I'm all for ideas and going for it, and with Danny and Toddy I've got people with the same enthusiasm as myself, and for the first time it's been me saying we need to take five minutes and think about it. That enthusiasm is gold, and you never want to dampen that, but at the same time in my experience in business over the years. I've never had to be the voice of reason. The minute you run out of ideas and creativity it's time to get in the box."

For those who don't know much about Colin or Futuresound Group and their web of inter-connecting businesses: it is essentially a loose collective of venues (The Wardrobe, The Key Club), festivals (Slam Dunk,

Live at Leeds, Get Together), promotions (Somewhere – a community of fans), artist management, record labels (Dance to the Radio, Slam Dunk Records, Tiny Library Records) and now, of course, a record pressing plant.

The myriad businesses are connected by overlapping business interests, but are all also fiercely independent, priding themselves on supporting new and underground artists. The Wardrobe, for example, is a multi-purpose arts space, bar and restaurant across two floors in the centre of Leeds'0 cultural quarter. Flexible in-house production means the venue can switch effortlessly between live music, comedy shows, club nights, DJ residencies and private events. Previous acts include Amy Winehouse, Catfish and the Bottlemen, First Aid Kit, George Ezra, Phill Jupitus, Charles Bradley, James Acaster, Craig Charles and Trevor Nelson. Flexibility is a common goal throughout all Colin's business endeavours, regardless of size, and is something he clearly thrives on.

Colin is also a very astute man and was happy to talk about what motivates him and, more importantly, what motivates him about his Press On investment. "With the promotion, the label, the management company, the bars, the festivals and everything else I'm involved in, I have managers. What gets me out of bed in the morning is not financial, but here I'd like to be here once a week if I can. I can question what the guys are doing or pat them on the back (because they don't do that with each other when they are caught up in the moment), plus my contacts in the industry is something I bring to the table. When we get the office finished next door I'll be able to come up here and spend a couple of days working from here and also help out with what is going on and be another pair of ears in the factory. I've got the enthusiasm and the vision so when they come to me with an idea about stuff I've either already thought about it or, if it's the right thing to do, I'll encourage it."

An investor like Colin would usually stump up the cash and then have little to do with the business, but with Press On he immediately wanted to input more than just finance. His hopes were that the relationship he was building with all the Press On staff would only get stronger and stronger as the business progressed. In his own words, Colin gets, "caught up in all aspects, so when the shit hits the fan…" but with his other businesses he admitted not looking over the shoulders of the managers: "I am the person that gets phoned and never when things are going really well. But I like to come up with solutions and work things out, and I think it helps the boys when I can say don't worry about it. It's not always a money thing; it's if we are jumping the gun. You'll always want to build a recording studio or get a cutting machine…"

Suddenly things were starting to make a bit more sense. Everything is in the timing, so when Danny first told me about their plans for the mastering suite and lathe, it wasn't open-ended optimism – it really was part of the Press On masterplan, albeit anchored by Colin's cautious experience.

However, Colin was not averse to running with the baton. "The thing about business is it's the way you deal with situations when everything has gone down and nothing's going out of the door. This is what it is like forever now for Press On.

"As long as you are in this business, it's [about] how you deal with the stresses and situations that arise. In May we had the printing problems, and then the galvanics with all the pops and crackles going on, and we had to strip everything back through a process of elimination to work it out. These things will always happen because when you are setting things up like a recording studio or getting involved in bio-compounds you are always going to be challenged, but the one thing that is important is that nothing is wasted in the process."

For all his easy-going nature and general affability Colin is almost militant in his pursuit of greener business practices and sustainability and, while Danny is equally passionate on this subject, one suspects it is Colin who is the real driving force in making sustainability an integral part of the Press On branding. Although he is keen to sell it as a mutual enterprise.

"The reason there hasn't been a new pressing plant opened in the UK for the last 30 years is not because nobody could be bothered, but because it's a really difficult thing to do and why I didn't do it ten years ago. But now we have the first one in the north of England. There are going to be problems, but not necessarily big problems as long as we come up with solutions and deal with it...

"Danny and Toddy are leading the way because we are not just setting up an off-the-peg pressing plant, we are doing it totally differently to how it's been done in the past. Things are different now; you can't go to an established pressing plant and say we are moving somewhere else or gut it and be really organised now. When you go to some of these factories, they're a liability because they've never moved forward.

"Once you start these machines pressing you can't stop if you are commercially driven, like most of the other plants are, and to an extent that will happen here eventually, but we've had time to organise and [create] systems, and the people that work here at all levels have all come up with a solution or an idea to help with that."

The idea that something can be made a couple of hundred yards down the road by someone somebody used to work with years ago is the spirit of being fair and being sound. And that permeates the very physicality of the business, from the walls of the building to the people inside it and, yes, even the Cuban flag still fluttering slightly in the rafters.

"Even if we were just doing Press On and nothing else, it would still be amazing. But we are not the type of people to leave it at that. We are not stupid either; we are not going to do things that are going to be detrimental to the business. Everything we do goes through a process. The business will become more departmental going forward to reflect that. I can imagine in the future FairSound having its own space somewhere in town, with completely different people doing that with a studio and somewhere you can go and have a sit down and speak to someone rather than doing it all online. So, there will be a team of people running that, another team running Press On and another running the bio-compound venture, but still integrated with the same directors, it will never be so big to be completely segregated.

"Then where does that go? Nobody wants to set up a cottage industry and just potter away. We are enthusiastic and want to make a difference in the industry. I remember the days when bands went on tour with their physical product released the week before, but now you are talking months after release date and the buzz is gone. I'm talking to artists at the moment about doing a vinyl-only release, not on stream or anything. Let's turn it around and not just limited run[s]: every few months you could have a recap on orders and just keep going because it will only ever be available on vinyl. Get A&R people creative about vinyl again, because the people upstairs [at the record labels] don't want to do it because it affects their relationships with the artists if it takes nine months to get the physical done on the release.

"The only way we can make a real difference is when we have six or eight machines pressing and that's the goal really, 1.5 to 2 million units per annum, which will cover most of the indie labels in the UK. The most important thing is to make a difference in the industry to make A&R people, company CEOs and Financial Directors turn around and ask why they aren't doing it on vinyl and doing it differently instead of it not being an option. Then I'll feel like we've made a difference to the industry…"

It was Colin's expert way of wrapping up the conversation, or perhaps his subconscious way with words, that really set the Press On Vinyl vision free. This was maybe something Danny and Toddy didn't always fully realise from the realities of the shop floor, and it was clear to me how much of an integral role Colin was playing in the day-to-day successes and challenges. Press On's ethos goes far beyond just removing the barriers to local, independent and unsigned artists. Not only does it want to revolutionise vinyl production, it wants to revolutionise how that vinyl is conceptualised not just at grass-roots level but also in the boardroom. Perhaps what they mean when they talk about FairSound changing everything…

Day 256
22 June 2022

Life got in the way, as it sometimes does. By early June, six weeks had passed since my last visit to Press On Vinyl and I was keen to see how things were shaping up in the live room and what Toddy had to tell me concerning his potentially big announcement.

What I found was a noticeable shift in mood. Not in a bad way, but there was a tangible seriousness that moved away from the banter-heavy manufacturing aspect of the plant and focused more on the marketing side. Toddy told me they had been pushed into taking stock on FairSound after a meeting with the spearhead of a large collective of independent labels that form a competing distribution network. Danny and Toddy had always said they would work for the greater good of the music industry: keen to share new ideas, but also careful not to step on the toes of others.

Decanting to the pub, Toddy opened up a bit more: "We've got three big artists who are probably going to release on FairSound. We are working loads with Ninja Tunes at the moment. And we spoke to another big independent label who wanted to build a plant before the pandemic, but they've fucked it off now for being too hard, so basically, they asked if we would we be willing to let them buy a machine. But that is not how it works here. So, they said why not build a separate plant? Leave this one as it is, service the people it is meant to service, and build another one and let them help fund it." This initially seemed about as far removed from the Press On Vinyl ethos as it was possible to be so I was surprised with what Toddy said next. "That's still not off the cards."

How it usually works is, large pressing plants will hand over a certain amount of capacity, equivalent to perhaps one or two machines running, to a larger independent label or one of the majors, in order to guarantee a certain level of turnover before they consider small runs for small or unsigned labels and artists.

Toddy took up the story, cautiously. "They already have capacity with MPO[35] in France and some of the other big people, but in order to see their growth potential they need even more capacity. The logical thing was to build a plant.

---

35   MPO's About Us section on their website merely states, "We are the most complete international list of the Vinyl Pressing Plants, Brokers, Lathe-cutting, and Lacquer Mastering Services. In our list you can find both small vinyl Lathe-Cutting companies that can cut and send to your granny one-off special vinyl dubplate with her favourite song, and the world biggest Vinyl Pressing Plants for vinyl release orders starting from 500 copies. We also provide you with the contacts of the Lacquer Mastering studios, where you can get a master record cut before sending it to the pressing plant."

They had the money, but they didn't have the people or the expertise, and now the machines are hard to get as well. We've got our connection with Franco and Man so we can get the machines. They could get the machines from Pheenix Alpha[36] or Viryl Tech[37] but it might take quite a bit longer and they would then have to take their best staff away to run it, leaving a massive hole in their retail operation. He was very forthcoming and said fair play to us for doing it and whichever way it works he is willing to fund another plant. So, that's the craic, basically."

Press On offered 5,000 to 10,000 capacity per month, in order to show their commitment to supporting the record label in return. With the plan to put on a third shift to go 24 hours a day in three weeks' time, capacity would be upped to about 3,000 a day, so not a massive ask for Press On, if a little off-script.

This company was a well-established record label on its own, but it also had a big e-commerce site and worked with a lot of other labels through that. It was part of a bigger association and was 50% owned by the group itself, so wasn't technically independent. But it retained, publicly, its independent ethos.

---

36   Pheenix Alpha has a convoluted timeline dating as far back as 1932 via various mergers and takeovers. The world's first fully automatic record press with computer control was introduced in 1972 by engineering firm Toolex and the AD12 quickly became the market leader. Having acquired Toolex at some point along the way the first modernised Pheenix Alpha AD12 was delivered to customers in 2016.

37   Viryl Technologies was founded in 2015 to manufacture and service a new fully automated and semi-automatic record press, with a plan to modernise the vinyl pressing industry. The company's flagship WarmTone™ press was introduced in 2016.

If this is all sounding very complicated and a little corporate, that is because it is, but Toddy was keen to focus on the positives of the meeting rather than the daunting possibility of taking certain bulls by the horns.

"What we learned from that meeting is that they are doing a lot of what we are doing in terms of helping smaller labels on their platform and trying to help them get pressing capacity. They want capacity, but it's not just for them, it's for all other labels. Ten percent of all new vinyl records get sold through their platforms. So, that kind of thing is not off the cards for us, but there has now been a bigger push towards the FairSound platform we always wanted to do.

"It's a very similar thing, but we are doing it from scratch – a sales platform with capacity behind it so artists can sell while they are waiting for the product to be made and then we distribute it to the fans directly so it's all in one, and that was the whole idea. It was parked for a while, but at this point in time we are looking more at pushing FairSound as just that."

Danny continues: "Press On needs to retain its manufacturing purpose, so that [it's] the name that is synonymous with that, but FairSound will still eventually deal a lot more with labels. The Music[38] haven't got a label but have got reach, so they will be able to use the FairSound platform to push the pre-orders to pay for the vinyl run. When we do that launch, we will do it alongside a couple of smaller subsidiaries who can't afford it all up front, and that will showcase what FairSound can do. But Press On remains the first access point."

---

38 The Music is a Leeds-based groove-led indie band who had recently played a big hometown comedown show and, at the time, were pencilled in as one of the names to help launch FairSound.

What Danny was basically confirming was that, for all the hyperbole of FairSound outliving and outstripping Press On in business potential, for now at least, it would be part of the Press On whole and not a separate entity. Of course, the option was there at any point for Press On Vinyl to take one prong of the fork and FairSound to take another.

It was clearly still a touchy subject though and, although not in disagreement, I could tell Danny and Toddy had found this decision a tough one, as they waxed surprisingly honestly. Perhaps they were still in two minds.

Toddy: "FairSound as a separate entity could be stepping on other people's toes. We have to make a final decision in the next week or two exactly how we market FairSound."

Danny: "Within about three weeks of coming up with the idea for Press On we already had the idea for FairSound, and although it hasn't quite come to fruition all of a sudden there is a great opportunity to do it the right way, because it makes no sense to start pissing off certain people for the health of the music industry as a whole."

Toddy: "Other plants and brokers have either seen what we are doing or are just offering [16-week lead times] for existing customers. Loads of people are not even releasing vinyl because of the delays. There are two main ideas for FairSound. One of them is the crowdfunding thing for artists who aren't 100% sure if they will have enough money to completely go ahead. They can crowdfund for anything from a month to three months, and then the lead time of 16 weeks starts. It is quite a while from start to finish, but they won't lose any money. The other thing we are looking to offer, but is still to be finalised, is for labels or people with a bit more money to pay up to test press point – lacquer, stamper and test presses, so around £500. Then you run the pre-order campaign for two months while the test presses are approved, then they tell us how many they want and at that point we order the labels and sleeves and schedule it in so basically during the 16-week lead time you've already been selling. Any pre-orders get distributed by us at a 10% commission, which is what you'd pay on Bandcamp. So, they are the two options we look like we are going to be launching."

Danny: "The point of FairSound has always been that anybody can access it and some people might say we've sold out by letting The Music use it, but I think the opposite, because it exposes what can be achieved if we offer it to all-comers."

Toddy: "Even the run sizes, we always said we would be more flexible once we got more presses."

Danny: "The reason we talked about small runs was to let people know we could do that, and that won't change as far as the Middlesbrough plant is concerned, but as we are now getting to the forefront of this industry in this country it's our duty to make Teesside the place where it's done. I see the building where we are now as being very chitty-chitty-bang-bang and anything more that comes from that will never affect the original ethos or the mad ideas that go in that colourful building." This reminded me of how Oli Heffernan and I had both likened the plant to Willy Wonka's Chocolate Factory, as if there was always something fantastical and too good to be true about everything. "It's the humility, and that building cannot ever change."

One thing I was keen to ask Danny or Toddy was about their extreme openness, which saw an almost constant stream of visitors to the plant for both commercial and creative reasons, an increasingly thorough social media document, and an ingrained urge to share their knowledge and experiences.

Toddy: "Our consultants have advised us previously that we shouldn't put so many videos online of our machines and we get that, but we aren't of this industry; we are new and this is us."

Danny: "We are up for the NE Business Awards, which was something I didn't want to do. We got asked to nominate ourselves back in March and we said no, but at the end of April they said we'd been nominated and could we send them 500 words for the bumpf. We sent them 20 which basically said, 'We are here to make records, we're here to make a difference, we've created a platform and now we are going to build on it'. Whether you like it or not we are shining a light on the music industry, but we are not going to be gung-ho and arseholes about it."

Toddy: "The uniqueness of our entry into the industry means we can put a different take on it and we don't owe anyone anything. Colin [Oliver] has connections going back 20 years that we don't, so we have the freedom to do that, but it also means we don't always know what we are on about! But there is a moral debate now. We'll just use this example: on paper, a record label is doing what we want them to do and that's great. So do we jump into bed with them [in terms of capacity], because they are already doing what we want to do? But then that feels like giving [capacity] away to an entity that might not deal with it in the way we want them to. Or do we push on and do what we are doing, but step on other people's toes? We are learning the complexities of the situation."

Danny: "We genuinely believe FairSound can change the UK industry, but we are tempering it to not compromise our ethos. I see it like a funnel and these next two weeks is about making a decision how we come out of the other end."

Throughout this earnest exchange, Danny, in particular, was in a formidable mood, sometimes standing to get his point across and then conversely switching to a conspiratorial whisper should anyone else be listening. Toddy sometimes smiled before finishing what Danny was saying, if in a more reserved way. Sometimes he just let him roll, still with a similar knowing smile. It was a routine honed over years of friendship and something that gave me a little more insight into what kind of banter went on at the plant when no prying eyes were watching. It was also a little bit of insight into what drives the two directors to succeed. The conversation also bounced all over the place: Twitch and Tik-Tok; punk as a historical and philosophical touchpoint; racism in music versus aggression in music. They could have literally gone on all night (and quite probably did, after I made my excuses and eventually left).

I told Danny I was originally from Durham and had only moved to Teesside for a girl about ten years ago. If anything, he was even more enthused as we discussed how everyone in Middlesbrough is an immigrant, a factor in the area's unique mix of accents. We talked about the old town and the industrial ghosts that litter the area. Relics of the past amongst a smattering of new developments. He regaled me with unlikely sounding but, I'm assured, totally true stories of railway lines under the river and the three Ridings of Yorkshire, and how the plant is situated at the boundary of the North Riding before, just as quickly, reeling off a list of influential names (past and present) in the local music scene and the importance of these people to him being where he is today, before going full circle and stressing, a kind of mantra of his, that there is no such thing an indigenous smoggy[39].

Toddy told me that Colin said to him ages ago that if Press On had been set up in London it would have been news for a week and then forgotten about. That is not to detract from Press On's achievements so far, just that everything gets swallowed up in the big cities. In Middlesbrough, however, Danny and Toddy had already been able to nurture an amazing family of staff through word of mouth and slowly building up a head of steam.

"We've never been on anybody's radar ever," Toddy said, "which is not necessarily a good thing, but it gives us an upper hand when we are trying to shake things up." Being very outgoing has its obvious benefits: Danny and Toddy have built up a wide range of contacts over the years through their day jobs, music side lines and social lives. Danny told me about Avenium Engineering, a stone's throw further along Riverside Park Road, which supplied parts for Rolls Royce and Nasa in the past, and which helped fix a problem in the galvanics lab just because they loved what Press On were doing.

While Danny was away at the bar again, I asked Toddy if the live-to-lathe concept was still on schedule. He said it was – but then he explained the hoops they were having to jump through to purchase the lathe from the well-known drum and bass mastering and cutting engineer in London who, for whatever reason, was selling all his cutting equipment. Everything was being accelerated to get things ready at the

---

39   Smoggy is a nickname given to people from Teesside, originally bestowed by visiting football fans, as these things often are, before being appropriated by Teessiders themselves.

plant for the lathe's arrival. That included arranging another engineer from Italy, who was one of only a few people in the world who knew how to put it back together.

With the finance in place, all £180,000 of it, and the Italian engineer's flights booked, it was squeaky bum time. Danny was maintaining that this was the best cutting lathe in the world and, if well looked after, would only go up in value. They were paying £30,000 more than they would have two years ago, but it could hypothetically run forever with the right care and maintenance.

"Neumann made these lathes, but the components don't exist anymore and the blueprints for the wiring are owned by one guy in Switzerland called Flo[40], who is a nightmare to deal with. People are trying to build new lathes but can't get anywhere near the same standard. Flo could, but he's just a very particular kind of character. One minute he'll help someone and then the next he'll just disappear into the mountains for a year.

"The main thing is we want to bring the whole process in-house. We control the sound quality, if there is a problem it costs us loads less to recut it and with our mission to provide live-to-lathe this is the perfect opportunity. Not only are we getting a lathe, we are getting the best lathe, but the guy we are buying it from holds all the cards."

---

40   Flo Kaufmann's Flokason offers the best hand-crafted audio equipment in Switzerland, but Flo is also one of the world's few lathe repair experts. He acquired the Neumann blueprints from Johannes Richter who was obliged by Neumann to offer ten years after-care on the final Neumann sales in the late 1980s, with Johannes determined to take the schedules and specifications to the grave. Legend has it, the pair worked together for a few years before Flo eventually won Johannes over and he eventually agreed to sell Flo a lathe.

Back from the bar, Danny began spewing forth about how scientologists bought up loads of cheap lathes in the 90s to record their sermons on, which ultimately led to the shortage. While there may only be some truth in this, there was certainly a sharp drop off in popularity after the mass uptake in CDs in the late 80s, followed by a general disregard for unwieldy and suddenly very old-fashioned vinyl. This led to many lathes and presses being scrapped or sold for parts.

Danny then returned to something we had earlier been discussing *off* the record.

"This stuff gets more difficult for us as we are dealing with bigger names in the industry, because we are *human*. Even as a kid, I used to wonder who stood on whose head to get where they were, and that is the reality of business. These are not easy decisions, but I can't think of one wrong decision we've made when having to choose between the moral right or the business right."

Maybe this is because, for Danny and Toddy, the moral right and business right are intrinsically paired somewhere deep in the synaptic soup of subconscious thought, informing their every move without them even realising. But Danny told me that the last month was the closest the pair have ever come to a proper row – even culminating in Danny having to offer Toddy a mid-afternoon can of Stella as something of a peace offering.

"It was unneeded really," Toddy later told me, "but I understand why Danny did it. I was on the phone so I couldn't even properly acknowledge that little peace offering. The amount of times we've come close [to arguing] you could count on one hand, and the amount of shit we have to decide, its mad. We've always disagreed on things, but the pressure now, at times, has been great. But we always sort it out after. Devil's advocate this, devil's advocate that and then we don't even dwell on whose idea we went with in the end. But I definitely haven't been able to provide the-chips-are-down fun lately."

Danny: "The reality of it is, we are definitely masking it at the moment. It all sounds mint on paper. We are still running at a slight loss, but it's the external pressure we put on ourselves because we realise what we have created, or sometimes people are manipulative from outside and all these things are like a cyclone. It's like when musicians suddenly make it – but at least we can see the snakes…"

Toddy: "It's not as plain-sailing as you think, and a lot of the weight is on our shoulders. It's rock hard. I wake up every day thinking I need to graft, couldn't work any harder and then go to bed thinking I didn't get done anything like what I needed to." I asked Toddy if he thought they were exhausted; not knackered from working long hours, but actually *exhausted*. "For the last two months. The way we work, the way we think, the way we are mentally. We can't go on much longer before one of us properly burns out. The burden of it all is on our heads."

In fact, the next time I spoke to Toddy he had just booked a two-week family holiday to Turkey and, while he had confidence in leaving the plant in Danny's more-than-capable hands, he did seem worried about it. I wondered how many of those long, late-night phone calls he and Danny would be having while he was away.

Both Danny and Toddy's wives also work at the plant and in fact it was their idea that I chat to them. So,

I caught up with Kerry and Emma together to talk about how the long, stressful hours affect them, their partners and their relationships.

By this time, the plant was running 24 hours a day, *five* days a week. Officially this was to allow the live and cutting room to operate on the weekends, but Kerry was quick to point out that for Toddy this meant he could keep his weekends totally free for family time, even if it meant often working very late during the week. But Emma was still worried.

Emma: "I think they both might still burn out. New things come up all the time. Just when you think they can chill, a machine will go down or there will be some issues with the galvanics. Todd is up until all hours working on his laptop and Danny has it on his mind all the time. He'll wake up at four in the morning. I get it a bit easier because I can switch off and have tea with James [Danny and Emma's son] and watch *Eastenders*, zoning out for an hour or two, which I don't think either Danny or Todd can do [so easily]."

Kerry agreed, admitting things still needed to change very soon with the pair's workload.

"One thing with Todd—" It's class that everyone at the plant can approach Director David as Toddy, but it is equally endearing the way Kerry and Emma clip it back to Todd. I wondered if Toddy and Kerry's kids even realised their dad's real name is David, "—is although he's working a lot, when he's home and with the kids he gives them his full attention and you can't even tell he's under that amount of stress. Also, if he explains what is going on at the factory," Kerry is part time while Emma is office manager so a lot more hands on, "I can understand more why he is working so late."

Emma: "Dan is the same. So many mornings a week he takes James to school and takes him to Cooplands on the way for a bacon sarnie, and they'll sit in the village and talk. Me and Kerry have got each other as well, so sometimes ask how each of them are."

Kerry: "Once Todd was really stressing and felt like giving all his shares away just so the company was safe and I didn't know what or how to help him, so I texted Danny to ring him. When one is high and the other is low, they help each other. They make a really, really good team."

Emma: "Toddy is really business minded, whereas Dan will be out on the floor and if something goes wrong he'll be straight in with some ideas. He's brilliant at talking to people while Todd is, well, he's Spreadsheet Todd! They never argue. I think if anything their relationship has got closer. They have their differences of opinion, but they don't fight; they'll always sit down and discuss it and manage to talk it out. The kids see each other more now as well, and they also come down [to the plant]... James went with Danny to Harrogate on Saturday to pick some sleeves up, and then they went out for lunch."

I thought back to the first time I met Toddy and how he told me, in his usual slightly understated way, about the family-oriented workers co-operative he had in his previous job on the foyboats, about how employees were automatically promoted to the board after a certain period of service, and how the company was really just a small cabal of families developed over a number of generations. It was easy to see the similarities already being forged here.

Kerry: "[Danny's son] James packs and Annie [Toddy and Kerry's daughter] goes round with her iPad editing little videos together. Our James [Toddy and Kerry's young son] likes playing with the PVC pellets. Although he's working loads and out late, Toddy's job before meant he'd be in and out all the time, so he'd only see the kids in bits, but now they are in school and we all have the weekends off they see him loads then. [Todd and Danny] are under a lot of stress, but to fix that stress they have got to come here still… Because it's all their mates and if it fails they they [would feel as though they have] let them all down. I would be so proud, but everyone has come here knowing it's a new business and it's a gamble. But the way it is going on with the stress levels, it can't continue… hopefully by Christmas they will have delegated more work, and the company is more financially stable which takes away a lot of stress. Emma was worried about that side of things."

Emma: "It's the phone calls and things when things go wrong, but it's also making sure people are kept in the loop. 99% are more than happy that at least you are telling them [if things go wrong], rather than us waiting for them to ring us."

Kerry: "I felt much better about everything after having a conversation with Todd about [their North American consultant] when he first came over. He had sat with Todd, discussed his workload, and told him to pass loads on to other people, in fact about 70% of his workload at that time [March]. When you start a business you do everything yourself because you know how to do it and then it takes some effort to teach someone else."

Emma: "When this room is finished they definitely need to move up here." We are sat in the still unfinished office space at the far end of the mezzanine corridor, immediately above the front door. A large corner window provides a spectacular panorama across the whole of TeesAMP, but even more spectacularly the Transporter Bridge is visible to the East, Newport Bridge to the West and the River Tees is just over the car park to the South West. It will make an equally spectacular boardroom in years to come, no doubt. A second internal window similar to those in the breakout room next door looks out over the factory floor. "They can see what is going on out there, and they will definitely go seven days a week when the next two machines come, and two more galvanics baths."

Kerry: "Sometimes Todd comes home and has to work all night because of too many distractions downstairs and *then* it impacts family life. But literally every day is different, anything from bad to amazing; it's like the whole Press On Vinyl process is just ups and downs. Being their wives, it's about supporting them because they are under so much stress, but they are following their dream which has also become our dream too. When they come home and they're stressed, I tell Todd to write a list in order of importance, but he always says they are *all* important!"

Danny told me later he was acutely conscious of putting too much pressure on the staff, because he understood how much they also care about them as people, colleagues and friends, and also their shared interest in the business and the fear of getting it wrong.

"We are putting things in motion around that. We want to empower people, but in the right way." By October the whole office was operating a lot more autonomously, with less weight on the shoulders of Danny and Toddy as the

Directors in the office daily, and many more decisions being made without their direct involvement. Anyone who has worked in a fast-paced workspace, whether an office or a factory, will know that kind of soft delegation is something often used by management to encourage staff to take responsibility and build confidence, while also improving productivity in the long term. From a management point of view, delegating some of the decision making meant many operational decisions could be made during one weekly meeting, freeing up much more time for Danny and Toddy to work on the longer-term goals of the company and, crucially, allowing them to take regular time away from the plant to spend time with their families and have something more of a normal life.

Toddy also agreed with what Kerry touched on, about how their North American consultant had set up a very similar business years ago and missed a period of his own children's upbringing by working ridiculously long hours at the expense of his family life and his own mental health. Toddy understood the importance of work-life balance more now and how important it is to put things in place, which is what Kerry had meant about delegation. "Some people would say, 'I'm the boss,' and do fuck all, so what we are doing is right. But being the boss and doing everything is not always right either."

We talked a bit more about the pressures of working with some high-profile investors, or at least associates that had invested quite large amounts of their own money, but Danny was keen to stress they all help each other out. Indeed, an example of that two-way street had happened the weekend before, when Colin Oliver's Futuresound had promoted a Libertines show in Newcastle. As Danny explained. "It's been tough at times and it's the engineering team that's got us through it, so I just asked if there was any chance he could get us tickets. No bother. He's part of the business. I'm going to buy [the engineering team] a few drinks and take them out for the day, and then the day before I asked him for *proper* guest passes to meet some of the bands. I don't think he gets us mad cunts, but I know if we succeed it will be one of the proudest things he's been involved in because he just thinks we are proper off it."

And we talked about the staff success stories that Danny was always so proud of. "Their success is not just Press On Vinyl's success; their success is human. There is an argument for everyone we employ becoming a better human."

I had the chance to speak to a few of them over the course of my visits. Kilvo, plucked from the daily mundanities of a grocery wagon job, recounted the Libertines jolly. He was already blasé about a little bit of VIP access, but he was still visibly excited about the VVIP access Colin had afforded them and how he even got the chance to swap a few words with Pete Doherty and then watch the band from just a few feet away. It was clear these kinds of occasional privileges were absolutely invaluable to staff morale. Particularly as this one came in the aftermath of a troublesome few weeks for the company.

Still in the pub, Toddy nailed it.

"Everyone cares like fuck."

Danny surreally likened it to a Scrabble board without any vowels where you can still make words, before Toddy continued in his serious tone. "One thing we've had problems with is machinery and some days I'd walk in full of beans and then see everyone's faces. 'Have you heard? The extruder's exploded again.' 'No, what's that mean?' 'It means we're fucked for three weeks.' Man built a very good product, but it wasn't fully tested. It could have gone the other way and not worked at all; but it did work – just with loads and loads of problems. Now [the machines] are working, but those problems delayed everything which put more stress on us financially and with the early orders. We've built a connection [with our stakeholders] and shown we are the first to back them, but it was a massive gamble and there were times we wondered if it would ever work.

"We went to a business event and we hate the stand-up-and-talk stuff where everyone just says 'We've had this much growth and got this much potential'. Danny just stood up and said, 'Right, it's fucking solid, we fucked up here, we fucked up there. Anyone thinking about starting a business just don't be afraid to fuck things up.' It was a whole talk about humility, and completely different to anything anyone would do at that event. It was absolutely class.

"Our focus is now switching more towards the business side of stuff."

I wanted to ask them about Press On's new Super Speedy Summer Special advertised on their Facebook feed, offering 100 records pressed in four to eight weeks for £699. It was the first time I had seen prices advertised online by them, away from the company website. It also looked like a direct response to other plants suddenly more focused on 16-week lead times, a very business-like move, especially the early July closing date. It was almost like a DFS summer sale. However, given what would come to light later it may well have been a last-ditch attempt to inject some much-needed cash into the business, or at least fill the diary to full capacity.

The offer was actually white labels (without centre label artwork – literally white labels), which meant the turnaround time could be reduced while ensuring a certain amount of capacity was reserved for print-free pressings, should there be any further problems like in May. Take up was steady, with 14 individual runs ordered. This, with the cash flow as it had been, was an invaluable safety net that probably helped Danny and Toddy sleep a little easier at night.

Day 260
26 June 2022

We reconvened a few days later back at Press On Vinyl HQ when the lathe had been delivered and was safely (still packaged and in parts) behind lock and key in an upstairs side room adjacent to its new home. The room it would be in was still undergoing an extensive refit, and a joiner was explaining a bit more about the soundproofing to Danny.

With a lot suddenly going on behind the scenes again I decided to spend a day at the plant to properly soak up the atmosphere, tie-up a lot of minor details with Danny and Toddy, and really delve into some of the more serious issues the plant faced now, nine months into their first year in business. Kerry was hard at work on the full hour-long documentary[41] they

---

41   Produced along with Dominic Dunn from Teesside University's

had planned, and was constantly tweaking the short clips that now fill the company's Facebook feeds. Danny never stopped all day and Toddy was, as ever, constantly on the phone.

A couple of nights before my visit, Danny, Emma, Toddy and Kerry had attended the North East Business Awards. It was a formal event, and although they may have confided to me that they were not too bothered about it, underneath the surface they were still proud to have been nominated, even after saying no when first asked to nominate themselves.

While on the night they may not have won an award, the victory was in already being considered for such an event. These sorts of businesses, these sorts of people, are not your normal nominees for these sorts of awards. Certainly not round their way.

As we walked upstairs for a scheduled meeting, I asked Danny about the stereo system they used for playbacks in the office, as I was curious how different equipment might affect the sound of the vinyl they were pressing. Earlier, he had been spraying some anti-static liquid onto Manchester post-punk band Ist Ist's new live pressing, to try and get rid of an annoying white noise that was emanating through the speaker, but was not in the groove itself. Ergo, the problem was in the pressing not the stamper.

Danny showed me a new sound booth they had recently acquired from Teesside University. At first glance it looked like nothing more than a conspicuous white box in the middle of the floor next to the staff break area, and a little like one of those flight simulator pods you used to get at theme parks in the 1990s. However, inside with the door

---

School of Computing Engineering and Digital Technologies.

closed, the noise reduction was almost palpable as Danny clapped his hands an arm's length away and I could barely hear it. The air acoustically dead.

The booth would replace the listening area on the factory floor. Back in the office, Danny was keen that this was another little step forward in the whole process of finding the perfect manufacturing environment for Press On's products. "Obviously we can come in [to the office] for playback but it isn't good enough. We've got mastering headphones out there [on the factory floor] but you still get background noise and there are visual distractions, so the booth will be where anyone on the shop floor who needs to do a quick audio listen or listen to a test press can go. Eventually any critical listening will be done in the mastering suite, which is going to be the absolute best listening environment, but we'll still need the booth even then, for anything we need to pause the press for."

The plan was that the booth would be fitted out in the same way as the external listening area on the floor, but would provide somewhere a lot more isolated for the engineers to playback test presses. Although most of the test presses to date had been fine, a couple had been sent out with sound problems, which was a worry for Danny. The new booth should eliminate any further mistakes.

"May was hard. We had a lot of orders to get out and we had some issues with orders being processed wrong or incorrect in some way, which was really stressful, and I took it on myself to do most of the difficult conversations. I wanted to protect the staff, but also give them an example of how to deal with those conversations because it's bound to happen. Toddy was the same, and that was a double dip, if you like, because all the money was spent."

Mayhem, it was now being called a few weeks later, after the dust finally settled. He confided that on top of the logistical problems with printing, which were outside of their control, they had also realised their computer systems weren't keeping track of everything, and at a point where they were already in full production. That potentially could have been disastrous. In fact, it very nearly *was* disastrous.

"Now there are loads of moving parts, the Enterprise Resource Planning (ERP) system we hoped would be built for us didn't work so now we've got a new one online." And once more for the layperson: "We had lots of different spreadsheets, which we realised wasn't good enough but we hadn't had time to sort it because of everything else, so we couldn't easily see how many orders we were taking for July, August and September. Then, when we checked, our cash was looking dodgy again."

The resulting realisation was that orders were trickling in a lot slower than expected because a lot of quotes were not being followed up on, meaning the company was only at 50% capacity for those months, which explained the sudden cash-flow problems.

"Now the sales are coming through better, and we've realised where we were wasting time and put more effort in and gone back to people and asked if they need more records or worked with them a bit more. Sales have increased, we've filled up most of the gaps [in capacity], and we've got loads more in the pipeline.

"It is looking better and if we weren't still finishing upstairs, trying to get more galvanics baths, and paying off the new machines that are coming, we would be about breaking even now. We are still investing, but by the end of the year I'd like to think we will be turning a profit. We were originally told we would get the first two presses in September last year and they would take a month to set up, but then we didn't really start pressing until the end of April anyway, so it was the first real stress test. A couple of people didn't get their records on the day they were expecting them, but we managed to do stuff for them like running off another 50 limited edition ones... As far as I know nobody has had a major problem where we have messed up a pre-order or anything."

For a new business, doing things in the nick of time is all part of the curve and is fine as long as it does get done. "If it has ever looked like we were going to be even a day late we would properly beat ourselves up, but we were still surprised how good people were when we talked to them about it," which perhaps says a lot about the previous state of the vinyl production market for small runs, and how easy it had been for Press On Vinyl to make strides forward quickly in some areas.

Despite Danny's assertions regarding the ongoing investment, the company was making money now in real terms and the business forecast would have predicted this point, but Danny admitted he found it worrying. "Every payday is stressful. We know we will always be alright, but you can't help not thinking about it because we have 20 staff and they're all our mates. It's unfathomable that they wouldn't get paid. Up until that point [of money worries] it was stressful, but more nervous anticipation."

A wiser man than me once explained the difference between good stress and bad stress, and that is what Danny was talking about here. Anything someone is passionate about should be stressful, but the difference is the anticipation of success against the fear of failure. Once the funds had been secured it was the anticipation of success – of waiting for the presses on Christmas Eve, then the lathe mini saga, the trials and tweaks of the galvanics lab, and now the sound pod – that drove Danny and the others. These are all good stress causes. With the money now spent, but the company producing regular revenue, they had effectively succeeded. So their focus moved onto financial sustainability and the stress of ensuring monthly cashflow, wages, stock control and the more mundane day-to-day business affairs such as rotas and sick leave. This didn't have to be bad stress, but it had the potential to feel anti-climactic after the euphoric highs of the previous few months, and this is the double dip Danny mentioned earlier. Not just a dip financially but, one surmises reading between the lines, a dip in mental health.

"Looking back now, there are things I think were hard," Danny said. "The galvanics department was very tough because it is so scientific. It's chemicals but it's also a biological process. You *grow* the stamper from a chemical, so it has an organic process. We still have the odd problem. We speak to Stamper Discs regularly. That's where most things with a detrimental impact stem from, the galvanics. Setting that up with minimal guidance was really hard, but because the pressing machines were delayed that meant it didn't really put too much pressure on us production-wise. It definitely contributed to the cash flow problems in May though, and there are loads of times with the galvanics where I have wondered what on earth we were doing. I've just been sent an article about us talking about it as if it is easy, but it is definitely not. It would be really difficult for experienced engineers to set up, so we've done a lot of learning.

"We were advised by loads of people not to bring that department in-house but if we hadn't, we would have been bankrupt by now because you can't source stampers as easily, simple as that. So a silly gamble, us being a bit cocksure, paid off, and once the cutting room is set up we can trace everything back to the original audio that was sent in.

"It cuts down on time, because if you do have a problem you can just get whatever you need doing again done, and it allows everybody to understand a lot more of the process as well. We want everybody to have an understanding of every department, not to understand *why* but to understand *how*. [North American consultant] advised against [the galvanics] and at that time he was right, because Stamper Discs would have been able to supply us, but even he said well done for not listening to him. Stamper Discs also said it would be difficult for us to do it."

This is certainly a good example of how quickly the industry has changed. In September 2021, when Toddy began speaking to Stamper Discs about them supplying the stampers, it was no problem, but by January 2022 they had no capacity left. By that point the Press On lab was well on the way to being up and running. "They wouldn't have cut us loose, but it would have been logistically hard. So, fantastic that we did it, from a learning point of view, and it also creates more jobs and brings new skills to Teesside."

From my seat in the upstairs breakout room that overlooks the factory floor, I could see one of the pressing machines was out of commission. Danny explained they were replacing all the seals on the hydraulic arm.

Danny admitted these two pressing machines were the first they could source. Other machines were on the market, albeit more expensive and with longer waiting times. It was another gamble, but this time a calculated gamble as Franco had 40 years' experience and Man had made numerous other machines. It surprised me a little that Danny was being so candid about this. Franco had previously been portrayed as a kind of galvanics God in the Press On backstory, sourced from the heavens (or at least picturesque Lombardy). He and Man have sister companies so it was common sense that, with Man already on board when they decided to go ahead with the galvanics, Franco would also join them.

"You can put this in the book." Danny stated firmly. "Franco made us a very generous offer, on very good payment terms, to take on the full lot." Even a cursory look at Franco and Man's business links online makes Press On Vinyl an ideal showcase for them moving forward together and when I suggested that, Danny was in no mood to be defensive. "It's a showroom and that is why we have had people over from Australia, Chicago, Poland and other places, but we were well aware of that when we agreed to the payment terms.

"I also think we've helped develop the machines because we've already made adjustments and we'll make further adjustments. They are basically prototypes which we have upgraded with their guidance. A gamble, but one we are very happy with."

It was interesting to hear Danny open up more about this kind of business arrangement. As a company, Press On had always celebrated the fact that people have come from far and wide to visit on the basis that they are doing something completely different with the set-up of the company in terms of sustainability, and focusing on independent artists and small runs. Knowing now that it is equally about the pressing machines and galvanics showcase also highlights what shrewd businessmen Franco and Man must be. Danny further explained how their freestanding model meant you could walk 360 degrees around the machines, while some other easy access features made maintenance, upkeep and quick troubleshooting a lot easier. Imagine being able to get to that annoying paper jam within seconds. Also, they are pink.

He said the mould on the pressing machines had a new carbon-coated surface that reduced surface noise when the record was played back, which was important to him. It was also verified by Lewis Hopkin at Stardelta Audio Mastering, which meant it was doing what it was meant to be doing. The technology combines CD manufacturing with record manufacturing.

Danny told me the lathe had arrived a week late because the previous owner, whether because of separation anxiety or not, simply held onto it until then. No reason or dint, that was just how it was. Danny was down in Birmingham with the Luton box van, dropping records off for the Commonwealth Games project and expecting a call to go to London the next day. That trip was called off at the last minute.

Danny had begun negotiations with the producer in November 2021, so it had been background noise for a while: "I was aware this guy had this fantastic business in London with two of the most sought-after cutting machines in the world and that he was going to get a lot of separation anxiety letting them go. The measure is, a piece of kit like that doesn't leave London to come to Middlesbrough. That doesn't happen."

Danny finally received the lathe the Friday before this conversation. Those in the know will be able to guess the finer which, who and why detail to this particular footnote in the Press On Vinyl story, but it seems churlish to dwell on a negative outcome for one party, even if it was to Press On's eventual benefit. It's certainly not something in the spirit of the Press On Vinyl ethos.

Danny told me Press On had to get financing to afford the lathe. We already know the company had a lot of debt at this time, and some of their investors were friends and family. That was something Danny always seemed acutely aware of, and perhaps the thing he found most stressful of all. As if sensing what I was thinking, he took a big breath and went on, "We can find a way to get more investment if we use equity or whatever, so as long as we have good foresight, then we will be fine. Once the lathe is set up we are going to have a pressing plant that is on a par with anywhere else in the UK for ability, for output, and also something for the North of England."

Furthermore, it was clear that events in May still weighed heavy on his mind. However, in true Press On Vinyl spirit Tommy had driven down to Torquay to drop some records off, Danny had been to London (twice) and Birmingham, Gareth had been to Norwich, and a small disaster had been averted. "Everybody we've done that for has turned round and said they've never had this off other pressing companies, it would [have been] tough luck basically. [The level of customer service] is important to us. A lot of the time [the delays weren't] even down to our doing; it was elsewhere in the supply chain. But it's our responsibility, ultimately."

Prior to this, Press On had worked with a couple of different distribution companies, but the longer-term goal now was to purchase a delivery van, which would go out two or three times each week with 500 runs or less on board. "Basically, anything that doesn't go on a pallet we are looking to deliver ourselves. It will be great for a couple of reasons: we can take better care of the records, because we've had some that got damaged, and it will also be great for the artists when they are getting the small run delivered if someone gets out of the van with a Press On top on, who has got a direct link to the company. It will really add an extra bit to that personal touch. And financially it would be viable. We might combine it with a packing job, so more of a distribution role. Greco Brothers[42] have always had their own delivery service and they are well established – you see their vans all over. But the most important thing for us is that the records get there in one piece. We've just had one today where there was some sleeve damage where they've obviously been shot[43] down, causing the records to slide and damage the outer sleeve.

"It's all part of our service, and rightfully so, so artists and labels at a small level don't have any toing and froing with a third-party distributor. Then, eventually, when we come into FairSound, the distribution to the artists' fans will be sorted out as well."

At this time all Danny would say about FairSound was that they were still looking at the best way to launch it. It would not be until my next meeting with Toddy the following month that I would hear about any real progress on the FairSound launch. However, the configurator had gone live on the website (something that apparently had been imminent as early as March) but Danny was hopeful FairSound would be launched in the next month or so. Danny's vagueness reminded me again of the 60-day countdown to nothing. For something as groundbreaking as I'd always been led to believe FairSound would be, with Futuresound's continued presence and no small amount of PR input from Hanglands, I would have expected something concrete in place already this close to launch. In fact, it would be October before the flagship platform was unveiled to the world.

---

42 Greco Brothers is a Middlesbrough-based family business specialising in ice-cream cones and wafers.
43 In Teesside parlance, 'shot' is used similarly to 'put'.

I later learnt that one of the problems at this time for FairSound was that presales would not be eligible for the vinyl charts. The chart system is set up in such a way that FairSound would need to report so many unit sales per month for six months before its sales became chart eligible[44]. Basically, as well as the regular Top 40 we are all familiar with, there are a number of other charts including dedicated singles and albums vinyl charts. Every physical sale from a registered distributor or retailer is automatically recorded towards the weekly chart position. Any private sales, or sales/presales by unregistered parties are not, therefore, chart eligible and the sale does not count.

The difficulty lay in persuading artists to use FairSound without the chartable carrot. Of course, Danny was already conscious of the fact there were other companies offering similar chartable services, and he was keen to find a way of getting some artists to use FairSound so it would be chart eligible as soon as possible.

He didn't seem overly concerned about that though. "The Music job is still on, but they won't be using FairSound, they'll be using Townsend in Birmingham – again, they can chart, and The Music want to chart. Every time a unit goes out of this building it still goes on the system and is classed as a sale, but it's not chart eligible. It's the same for record shops if they haven't gone through the same process. I understand it, but I think there has to be a better, quicker way of getting people on board."

It's easy to empathise with Danny's frustration with this, especially when vinyl sales, particularly 7" vinyl, are still sufficiently low for small runs to be able make a significant

---

44   UK chart rules can be found on the Official Charts website.

impact on the vinyl chart. One thousand 7" sales in a week is often enough to vie for the top spot. Savvy artists with this in mind might initially shy away from FairSound until it is chart eligible, but then how does it become eligible without any artists on board? Danny is always one with a metaphor. "It's like applying for a job when you have to have experience. Well, how do you get experience without being given a job?"

However, for all these irritations Danny was clearly still as fully invested in the FairSound model as he always had been, and in how it would revolutionise how unsigned artists and small labels do business. "Artists can [run a] pre-order campaign, so their fans will pay for [the pressing]. Labels, as well. Butterfly Effect[45], for example – I'm sure there are probably times their cashflow is tight and it would be much more beneficial if they could do a pre-order campaign online and at least get the money to cover the costs of the run. It will still be pay upfront: we will be able to help people a little bit, but it's still 50% upfront and 50% on approval of test presses. That is where the industry is at.

"We had a really good label the other day asking about further discounts, and we can't, because we would have no more profit left and where we are at now, we need to start getting as much revenue in as possible. As we build relationships, we'll look at ways we can maybe get them some better payment terms based on a year's worth of projected orders, maybe. It's the same for us though. We have to pay cash upfront for our PVC for at least the first ten big orders."

---

45   The publisher of this book, Darlington-based Butterfly Effect, is a record label specialising in carefully curated limited vinyl releases and arranging events featuring their favourite artists. This is Butterfly Effect's first book.

As I was leaving for the day, Danny handed me a record they had pressed recently that he was clearly particularly proud of: a beautiful yellow vinyl compilation album especially commissioned for the 2022 Commonwealth Games in Birmingham and featuring Brummie legends UB40, as well as The Friendly Fire track, 'It's a Brum Ting', which was chosen by the BBC for their coverage of the games. The fact that Danny was so thrilled that the Press On Vinyl logo was included on the liner notes of the gatefold sleeve along with Arts Council England and the National Lottery Heritage Fund just showed that Press On Vinyl will never stop being exciting to him. (Next time I saw Danny socially, at a gig, we got chatting about my lapsed support for Newcastle United caused, in part, by the unethical takeover of the club. He wanted to stress he didn't agree with the Commonwealth Games per se. It was the most Danny thing to say, but not something that really needed to be said.)

Day 270
6 July 2022

I had heard on the grapevine that there had been a big meeting in early July that had left many staff members feeling exasperated and concerned about their futures. Then, when I next arrived at the plant at 10am on a Saturday morning for another pre-arranged meeting, I found it strangely deserted. When Danny did arrive, he looked tired, but I shrugged it off as an Un-Convention[46] hangover, as he had just got back from Manchester the night before.

When I put it to him later about the meeting and how tired he had looked, he seemed a little taken aback, perhaps at how much non-verbal information I had been able to

---

46 Founded in 2008, Manchester's Un-Convention is a series of music conferences, showcases and events to share ideas and discuss the future of the independent music sector.

pick up from my visits, but I decided to leave it there on this occasion.

Danny was perhaps a little jaded after a couple of run-ins with other ventures trying to do similar things as Press On, but also a major label who, he told me, didn't want the vinyl market to grow any more than it already had.

The label in question had apparently recently missed out on a Top Ten chart position because of problems getting the vinyl out on time. We are again reminded that the format-less format continues to be the industry's preferred method of delivery solely to maximise profits, rather than supporting other formats for other people.

Danny did say, however, that FairSound had been well received generally, and was currently being beta-tested by Manchester band Fuzzy Sun and Brighton-based Opus Kink. While Fuzzy Sun failed to get their assets over in time, Opus Kink would be joined by Butterfly Effect, Love'n'Joy and local indie-house pioneers Vanderbilt, amongst others. So, while the big-name endorsement from The Music may have been missing, it was still full steam ahead with the platform. Colin also told me his long-term vision was a completely separate town centre site for FairSound, where artists would even be able to walk in off the street to find out more about the products or get a quick quote.

For a town like Middlesbrough, struggling with lots of empty units and anti-social behaviour, this struck me as either visionary or foolhardy. But the more I imagined how this kind of venture might revive a whole street it was located in, or even create a brand-new micro-scene, the more I was on board.

Nevertheless, some trouble up at the mill, perhaps...

Day 299
4 August 2022

With the country seemingly over the worst of a record-breaking heatwave, when I next returned to the plant in mid-July I was pleasantly surprised to find the cutting room all but complete, although the lathe itself was still under lock and key.

At the time of my visit Theaudience[47] were riding high at number four in the vinyl album chart, just behind Harry Styles and James Bay, with another record pressed in Middlesbrough – a re-pressing of their only album.

On site, the mood also seemed more settled after Mayhem, as it was still jokingly called, partly to preserve their own sanity, one suspected. Some knock-on effects were

---

47   Readers of a certain age will remember Theaudience as being the band Sophie Ellis-Bextor was in, pre-Groovejet fame.

still being felt, Toddy would later confide to me, but things certainly seemed back on an even keel, at least on the surface. Thoughts had turned again to sustainability and the longer-term success of the plant while maintaining the ethos I was still hearing so much about.

The live room downstairs still needed boarding out and soundproofing, and there would be some more sound-absorbing midi walls going up:

"We'll be able to record as soon as it is properly finished, but live-to-lathe depends how quickly we get good at the cutting and up to speed with that new skill set," Toddy told me. I found Alex and Uncle Nige hard at work downstairs using what would eventually become the live room as a kind of woodwork shop, as they prepared all manner of wood and hessian designs that would provide the mastering suite upstairs with custom, state-of-the-art soundproofing, for almost perfect sound quality in the suite itself. They would create a futuristic sonic hub lined with these acoustic panels to exact specifications, like egg boxes but much, much better. In mastering, nobody can hear you scream.

Toddy was also excited to tell me about another interesting development involving a little label called Worm Disco Club. "They run a cool thing at Glastonbury and all over. They are mint, and they supply their own lacquer. Usually we supply the lacquers, which at the minute we are out-sourcing, either that or about 15-20% of our orders know the studio they want to cut it so they supply their own that way," Toddy had given Worm Disco Club their test presses, which they were really happy with, but they had also sent them to Lewis at Stardelta Audio Mastering. Toddy admitted he had been shocked to find out Stardelta operate on a scale and pedigree comparable to Abbey Road and Metropolis and are one of the top cutting studios in the country. There, Lewis Hopkin had produced in Toddy's words, "quite a long report, some good and some bad. He said we were not far off considering we were new, but he spotted a few things."

Lewis basically looked at the whole record under a microscope, taking pictures and listening to every groove. This enabled him to diagnose problems firstly by what he could see in the groove itself (including a build-up of certain things caused by silver in the galvanics) or in the actual pressing that might impact on sound. "Obviously there is stuff we know, but there is stuff he can see we haven't even got round to learning yet."

Long story short, Lewis' final conclusion was that if Press On were happy to go ahead with the release they should, although he was on the fence in terms of quality. In true Press On style, Danny asked if he could speak to him personally about it and, in typically Danny style, a few hours later, he came off the phone having agreed to send Lewis a further five records the plant had pressed. Some of the worst, some of their best and some in between and, crucially, without telling him in advance what the issues were and which were which. They also included one that they thought was as near perfect as possible. The ultimate blind test and not something someone in Lewis' position needed to do. Lewis had produced a huge report on all of the records, and that is where Toddy took up the story:

"The problems were mainly on jobs where lacquers were supplied from places we don't usually use. This meant we had been second-guessing our processes at times, and blaming our stampers for audio and cutting issues. But the nuts and bolts is, [Lewis] analysed a lot of stuff and spotted a lot of good things we are doing and a lot of things we need to change. Because of that it's more important than ever we get our own cutting up and running."

Naturally Stardelta agreed to help, though as these things always seem to work, Lewis and his team were also moving into galvanics, so Press On would help with that. Quid pro quo.

"He's now sending us cuts, we are making the stamper and sending that back along with the test press and the full press, and he's going to analyse it all. We've got a good partnership with him to make things better here. One thing he said was that he's never heard surface noise and low-end rumble lower on one or two of our pressings, and he's only ever used a German company before who were regarded as one of the best in the industry. He also said there's something different about these pressing machines."

While the first two pressing machines are essentially Man's 360 Allegro II machines, the tweaks that have been made have seemingly added something extra nobody can quite explain in the quality of the presses they produce.

"He's an absolute fanatic. He's mainly cuts, but he's also been involved in pressing and knows it inside out, and he's been waiting to find a pressing plant in the UK who he can work with. He's done a lot of drum and bass mastering and cutting using Optimal Media in Germany, but because of Brexit it's become a nightmare so now all that work will come through Press On. He thinks by the end of the year we'll be pressing some of the best vinyl in the world. It has literally put under a microscope what we are doing."

Now seemed like a good time to ask about the other two pressing machines which were supposed to arrive by August, and I was a little surprised by Toddy's answer. He told me they were meant to be getting *shipped* by August but would now be getting shipped in early September to arrive by October. "They are the same machines as the two we have, but they will be yellow and black, and we will probably brand them FairSound to show clients we have capacity specifically for that."

The first week in August also saw a flurry of activity on the Press On Vinyl Facebook feed. A 'Vinyl Odyssey' blog feature had been added to the company website, featuring Neil and Steve on a tour of their favourite vinyl record stores in the North. The first visit was to Stockton's Sound It Out, and the blog would later feature Black Slab in Redcar and Vinyl Eddie in York amongst others. Kerry also shared a link to Platinum Print's[48] mesmerising gluing and folding machine. When Tommy had told me what a good rapport he had built with the printer they were working with, this was obviously what he meant. It was also clear why Danny would be so cheesed off about sleeves being damaged by undue care on the part of delivery companies after so much care had obviously gone into their production as well as the vinyl itself.

Elsewhere online, part one of the five-part mini-documentary series Kerry had been painstakingly editing on one of my earlier visits got its first airing. It featured Komparrison recording their EP at Blue Bridge Studios, in the shadow of the Transporter Bridge, and The Music showcased the pink vinyl version of their new live album also pressed in Middlesbrough (though not now in conjunction with FairSound, as originally planned).

On 6 August, I attended Twisterella's Class of 2022 showcase event in Middlesbrough Town Hall's beautiful

---

48 Established in 1988, Harrogate-based Platinum Print is a multi-functional printer specialising in graphic design, packaging and distribution.

courtyard. In the build-up, a Press On Stereo Spesh on the company social media accounts featured all eight bands on the bill. The line-up included the cream of new Teesside talent, a couple of James Arthur's ex-bandmates, and headliners ZELA. While I knew Danny was friends with the promoter of the event, it was a nice touch of his to help promote the day. In fact, I bumped into Danny there. It was cool to have a couple of drinks outside of usual book business, but it was also obvious something big was being cooked up in the background. The following week, the slightly cumbersomely named 'Twisterella Build Up Special Press On Office Stereo' playlist was announced, exclusively featuring Twisterella artists. The playlist would be added to weekly until the festival itself on 8 October.

While metropolitan music festivals might be one of the great grass roots developments of the last 20 years for independent music, Twisterella, founded in 2014, has already ingrained itself into local tradition and outgrown the local music niche. It seemed the perfect place for Press On to announce what might become the next evolution of the regional music scene while also impacting on the way the music industry operates further afield.

Day 325
31 August 2022

By the end of August a few other things started coming to fruition. It felt like phase one of Press On Vinyl was starting to come to its natural conclusion. Toddy had told me about various ways of making vinyl production cleaner, from ways of recycling waste more effectively to using a brand-new bio-plastic alternative. He had also told me (off the record, at the time) about Press On's continued involvement with Middlesbrough's Twisterella festival.

The big news now was that FairSound would be officially launched at Twisterella festival on 8 October. I had already noticed that the updated festival poster included a new sponsorship logo reading 'FairSound powered by Press On Vinyl' and Toddy confirmed this when he told me they would be attending the festival's flagship Unconference on the morning before the main event to give a talk about the FairSound platform. They would also be providing a shuttle bus to and from the plant for anyone that wanted a quick tour.

"We sponsored a stage last year and buzzed off it, and they buzz off what we are doing here too so we were already going to sponsor a stage again. We were also going to do a talk at the Unconference in the morning about FairSound, but we are now pushing for that to be fully ready by then so we can announce that it is launched that weekend online. We checked whether they minded because the last thing we want to do is take any attention away from Twisterella itself, because it's unbelievable what they do, but they loved the idea."

Not only would Press On Vinyl sponsor a stage as 'FairSound: Powered by Press On Vinyl' but they would curate the pre-party on the Friday night at Play Brew. Play Brew had initially asked to be involved in the festival, but they couldn't be, really, as they are too far out of the town centre, near the Newport Bridge. They were given the pre-launch event by the festival promoters, which Press On Vinyl agreed to fund and pick the headliner for. Then FairSound would go live on the Saturday. The plan was still for small groups to visit the plant if they wanted to, and Toddy joked that Tommy had already been roped in to be the entertainer on the bus, "Tommy Bingo."

The whole time we were talking Tommy was hard at work next to me but hidden behind his large computer monitor, and so uncharacteristically quiet I had completely forgotten he was there until he concurred with a "no problem" in a pitch-perfect Sean Connery impression.

The mastering suite and cutting room would also all be wired up by then, and Toddy still had hopes for the live room too. "Maybe not exactly how we want it, but it will technically be able to have people jamming and recording in there when they come on the day, and we might have a DJ in the plant and someone running a press. We've also talked about doing some test pressings on the day for some of the FairSound pressings that will be coming out afterwards, maybe Love'n'Joy. FairSound will be what it always was, which was an artist platform for sales, pre-orders, funding and direct-to-fan distribution. Records to start with, but ultimately all merch and digital distribution."

On 23 August, Press On shared a post from Evolution Music announcing the world's first bio-plastic vinyl record alternative. If a big green announcement from Press On HQ was needed then this was certainly it. The two-minute clip explained how the vinyl is made using plant waste and can also be disposed of in industrial composting, while sounding as good as, and being marginally more durable than, a traditional vinyl record. Evolution Music had teamed up with Blood Records to fully test the product on the market and an example record spun around for the camera with the bright pink Press On Vinyl label clearly visible.

On 1 September, Press On followed this up with their own announcement and a video featuring Danny and Graham Cotton, Head of Sustainable Product Innovation at Colloids who, as the company that make the compound, are the Material Partner for Evolution Music. As the team set up the machines to work with the new material, Graham explained that it had different temperature and melting profiles to traditional vinyl. But with the new accumulator tank up and running behind the wall, it was relatively easy now to adjust the temperature and pressure accordingly. Although, as with the previously untested pressing machines

Franco had supplied, a certain amount of trial and error was to be expected.

Press On's socials had long since become busy digital highways. The Evolution Music link up was another in a long line of successful partnerships made even stronger by Ninja Tune (another long-time affiliate of Press On Vinyl) agreeing to let Bicep's[49] stamper be used for the first test pressing. This would ultimately lead to a record featuring Michael Stipe, no less, that the team would be immensely proud of. A record that might be revered in years to come as a genuine game-changer in how records are produced and sold. That was the plan.

---

49   Bicep are an electronic music and DJ duo from Belfast whose *Isles* album was released on Ninja Tune in 2021, to rave reviews.

Day 335
9 September 2022

It was already the first week in September and as the children returned to school for another year, the weather was turning autumnal, trees already with leaves on the brink of browning. As for Danny, not one to be distracted by such trivialities as the changing of the seasons, he was champing at the bit to tell me what had been going on since my last visit. Behind us a steady stream of hot-off-the-press vinyl was playing, as the back shift tried to iron out some little galvanics problems that had crept back in of late.

First things first: the bioplastics announcement. In terms of Press On's ethos and pledge to keep moving forward on sustainability, came at the right time. The plant was now running comfortably 24 hours a day, five days a week (with weekends still saved for recording and any emergency cuts). With the FairSound announcement imminent, the extra capacity afforded more time to fully engage with these kinds of developments – something one suspects would not have been possible even a few weeks previously. Another case of Press On's stars aligning.

Of course, the product had already been tried at various plants around the world, with varying degrees of success. Danny handed me a test pressing, explaining the record I was holding was made entirely of sugar and starch. I slid the disc out of its disco sleeve. It looked very much like a vinyl record, if a little smoother looking to the eye, with a strange sort of sheen to the surface. I would later learn this was due to a secondary mould release compound, which rises to the top during heating to literally help release the mould from the record once it is pressed, giving the record an unusual sort of cloudiness.

The backstory was that Evolution Music had been working on the bioplastic product for four years. Toddy had spoken to them on and off for a couple of months, but nothing concrete had come of it. Then they rang up, out of the blue, to say they had been running a job at another pressing plant in the UK without getting the desired results and could they give it a try in Middlesbrough. "That was the Thursday. They came on the Monday, and we pressed it the same day with mint results. We had got permission from Ninja Tunes to use the Bicep stamper and their audio people (Blood Records) have also been saying they can't believe how well it has been done."

And that, essentially, is how the world's first commercially available bioplastic record featuring Michael Stipe and Beatie Wolfe (and produced by Brian Eno, no less) came to be. "As it stands, it's the first bioplastic record that has gone to market, so it's the world's first sellable bioplastic record, and it sold out in four hours on the EarthPercent Bandcamp page."

A further footnote to this particular anecdote, and true to Press On's continuing aim to please at any cost: Evolution Music had asked for some test presses to arrive before they went to the Making Vinyl Conference in Germany in September. Danny said they could press the test presses, but that they had no chance of getting them to Germany because of the pressing schedule and the postal strikes in the UK at the time. In the end, Danny booked a flight, flew them over and dropped them off at the conference himself. If that isn't end-to-end service I don't know what is. Surely everyone lapped it up... "We expected a lot of push back from [the bioplastic record] to be honest, from people in the industry. There was a little bit, but the majority of people we spoke to were excited about it."

For those who have known Danny since long before Press On Vinyl, this commitment to green issues will be no surprise. His effervescent, laddish charm may verge on brashness at times, but it masks a selfless, thoughtful interior. Way back in 2010, Danny was running a food company called The Homemade Soup Van which won Green Business of the Year locally, mainly because all his food was made out of corn, while his packaging and utensils were all recyclable and compostable, something of a revelation at the time.

"We got the piss took out of us back then, but I've always been passionate and seen that there is a future way in doing things. The change won't happen overnight, but to not be part of it moving forward is naïve for such a new facility like we are. We already believe in it. I'm also a music fan and you can't beat vinyl so without trying to get there you never will."

The new bioplastic records were only possible because they are able to be pressed on existing pressing equipment. Any deviation away from existing hardware, at this stage at least, would render the project impossible, but I wondered about the strict environmental conditions and temperature constraints in the factory, and how that might affect the longer-term logistics of producing more expensive bioplastic versions of records.

Press On had been advised to press the bioplastic at a slightly lower temperature, but in the end were running close to normal temperatures as the parameters in the timing of the press were being tweaked instead. That meant the temperature didn't need adjusting as much. In fact, there is an argument for not heating the mould if the bioplastic puck itself is hot enough, because the compound is so malleable compared to the PVC (which goes hard quite quickly). However, for now Danny was happy just to be able to press a ground-breaking new product without any obvious loss in quality.

"It's good. In my opinion, it's about 85% there in terms of sound quality. Evolution Music, because of the journey they have been on, are saying it's 95% there. Whichever way you look at it that last 5% is always the hardest anyway, if you are going for sonic perfection.

"Personally, I still think a normal music fan with no sonic expertise could tell the difference. It sounds like a wind is blowing through it. Because of the mould release you can't see the grooves as much and it will bend and warp easier. I don't know if we are just dead critical because we are listening to lots of records all day, but it definitely doesn't interfere with the audio. There are no differences in pitch or frequency, it's just like there is a layer on top of the audio and it's not normal surface noise, either. So, we think that is the mould release compound that stops the bioplastic sticking to the stamper. Even now they are developing another new compound with talc in it. It's a massive success so far and dead exciting to be part of it."

To get to this point Evolution Music had tried a number of other pressing plants, some with very experienced engineers and sound experts, but they were apparently met with quite a bit of resistance from vinyl purists. However, far from being an afterthought, it seemed the Press On partnership was in part cemented by Danny et al's commitment to sustainability and eco-friendly alternatives.

"We are going to be a formal partner now with Evolution Music, and they have already had 400 enquiries on the back of our test press. We will get all the work and a head start on using the new compound."

In fact, Press On were already in early discussions with Evolution Music to create a sustainable sister plant with the raw products, essentially food waste, processed on-site. This could be another world first, and a massive research and development coup for TeesAMP and for Teesside, with positive ramifications further afield both inside and outside the music industry.

While the price per unit may be prohibitive at present for unsigned DIY artists, Danny was confident that once demand is high enough there is no reason unit price shouldn't come down to the same as PVC, and without the ethical challenges of having to dig oil to get it. Furthermore, Evolution Music apparently already had something in the pipeline with one of the biggest food suppliers in the country to get all the raw product they needed. Indeed, a fully sustainable plant could prove to have a positive impact on the environment. Danny said this pipe dream might be five to ten years down the line, but without starting to look into it now, how would it ever come to fruition?

"If they can get [the bioplastic] that good, they could use it in aviation, because they use more plastic than the record industry. I don't think Evolution Music could believe how open we were [to the concept]. But it's no good just us being able to do it. We want to teach people how to do it as well, not charge for it either, just publish it online. We don't want to come across like we want to save the world, though, so we'll just let other people shout about it." Which explained the Facebook share rather than the big 'I am' when the game-changing link-up was first revealed. "But we will offer this service as part of FairSound.

"In terms of unit price, what we have advised them to do with the Michael Stipe one is [rather than a sleeve] get a disco bag in recycled material and just put a sticker on. Yes, the unit price of the disc is higher, but cut back on the packaging to get somewhere near cost wise and it would look really cool, too, with a 90s nightclub sort of vibe, but top end."

Ever the music fan, I couldn't help noticing a Bob Dylan record on the table too. "That's for a magazine which they stopped making because they couldn't get the records pressed, but they've started up again now." I thought about an earlier visit where there was some excitement about the Low Hummer presses that had first used the slow cooker to good effect while Sweetie was packaging some Charlie Simpson albums, and how far things had come since then. No disrespect to either Low Hummer or Charlie Simpson, but we were now legitimately talking about Michael Stipe and Bob Dylan releases being pressed in Middlesbrough.

Apart from Tommy's constantly reassuring one-liners and Elise's infectious enthusiasm for *everything*, it was the rest of the staff's courage of conviction in approaching the Directors of the company even while they were obviously in a meeting that often struck me. Now we were interrupted by a particularly keen engineer wanting Danny to listen to a yellow vinyl they had just pressed out on the factory floor. My interest was piqued. One thing I had learned from my visits to Press On Vinyl was how different coloured vinyl reacts to the pressing process and as Danny carefully placed the vinyl on the turntable and let the needle drop, even to my untrained ears there was a lot of static on the playback. "Yellow is notorious. Black PVC is perfect for the job, it hasn't been interfered with, it hasn't been made to be anything other than a compound for making records. It's the colour that it is when it comes out of the ground."

Truthfully, I'd never given any thought whatsoever as to why vinyl records have historically, apart from limited runs, been universally black. If you hold a really well-pressed black vinyl up to the light, you should be able to see some of the colours of the spectrum in it, like seeing an oil splash on the road, as all the natural oils rise to the top. Basically, as soon as you start trying to make the record a different colour, you are adding things to the detriment of the sound. Press On had previously scrapped (read: recycled) 800 yellow pressings for that exact reason. The label involved had approved the test pressings so obviously asked why they weren't sending out the final presses and Danny went straight to the point: "Because it sounds shit."

They did, however, send a few to Lewis at Stardelta to analyse. His view was that Press On should have sent them out, as the only problem with the run was that it was bright yellow, and you expect it to have that sort of noise on it. Validation. Of sorts. But for the record, yellow vinyl really is shit.

"Don't get me wrong," said Danny, quick to reassert the company position and waving a pristine blue King Gizzard & the Lizard Wizard[50] record at me that I hadn't noticed on the table before, "we've passed some fantastic coloured records. This sounds awesome – so it can be done."

A constant on my late summer visits to Press On Vinyl was Danny or Toddy's keenness to show me how the live room and mastering suite were coming along, which was often underwhelming. Mainly I saw lots of wood and tools in various states of construction and abandon, but by late August things were really starting to take shape.

"This is going to be the live room–" which I already knew, because he'd already shown me it three or four times, but the way Danny waved his arms, almost regally, told me he thought it wasn't a million miles off now "–and we've *just* booked Opus Kink to record the first live-to-lathe recording on 21 December." It still looked like a house extension without carpet and plaster to me, but one thing I noticed was

---

50 Interesting aside: King Gizzard & the Lizard Wizard don't copyright any of their records so anyone can bootleg them. The record Danny was waving at me was for a label that just decided to press a live album of one of the band's gigs without any permissions or royalty arrangements.

the acoustics and Danny even did a little shriek for effect, as if reading my mind. The sound in there was going to be *loud*. "This is a beautiful by-product really, it's going to be perfect."

Upstairs, the cutting room was heavily padlocked but Danny assured me the lathe was set up behind the fortifications, which were perhaps understandable given the cost and delicacy of the equipment in there. However, the mastering suite, which previously had been a shell of a room, was now an Aladdin's Cave of half-finished wood and hessian constructs, which had been in the workshop-cum-live-room but now expertly hung in all corners of the room, creating a similar crisp muffle to the way the sound carried in the sound booth downstairs on the factory floor. A plush leather sofa was at the back of the room, as one would expect in any state-of-the-art studio, while at the front desk Alex was on a call about the console they would be installing, but already partly surrounded by a large, curved desk with pop-up speakers either side of him. Like a vintage wooden sports car with pop-up lights and some other very high technical specification equipment and gadgets.

"We were advised to do a singer-songwriter for the first live-to-lathe, but we thought fuck that!" Danny laughed and then showed me down to the factory where some of the floor staff were trying out various different marble effects for a release by Manchester experimental rock band, Ist Ist.

The sound booth was now decked out in Denon and Pioneer separates, while some PA speakers now allowed the records to be played out on to the factory floor, purely for pleasure. On a serious note, the sound in the audio booth is so muted, my audio recording of my conversation with Danny had barely picked up anything when I played it back.

As for FairSound, Danny confirmed it would be launching on 7 October, with socials going live the following day. "The website is about done and the people we've got to beta test it are ready to announce. Opus Kink are one of them. They are going to do a 12" single."

But for the rest of September, there was no mention of FairSound from Press On. They were just promoting Twisterella on their socials. The carefully planned media blackout was to allow full exposure for Twisterella and all the other related media to go out the week before the festival itself on 8 October, and then just say (in Danny's words again) "we are launching FairSound tonight and that's it".

"We don't want to overshadow Twisterella, and there will be a lot of chatter about it afterwards so it's pointless having a big lead into it. The people we've got to beta test it will get it to the national press anyway." Danny suddenly sounded a lot more press savvy than the guy I first met nearly a year before. "But we are pleased Twisterella have let us do this that weekend. It's about Boro, and that's why we want to do it that weekend. We love Twisterella. We always said about this Detroit thing [which Danny first mentioned way-back-when at the beginning of this book], and that mastering suite upstairs and being able to record live-to-lathe is going to be the start of it; having more venues and places that are better to have gigs will be next…"

The launch would be at Play Brew Co, which, although deemed too far from the main festival to be directly involved, was still something of a coup for them and their team, who also strive endlessly to support local creative endeavours. Danny, however, was not happy about another issue surrounding the launch. "We are still hoping Love'n'Joy will play, but fuck me getting their visa is proper embarrassing. They've been to 17 countries in Europe, but to come to England it's going to cost them £3,500 which they won't take in gig money. They pretty much have to say where they are going to sleep, how they will afford to eat. [The government] want to know exactly what their expendable income is. It's ridiculous. I had to write an invite letter explaining exactly why we want them to come, and I felt a bit encroached on myself. Why the fuck should we have to explain ourselves and exactly how it works? It's culture. We are making this thing happen and we want them to be part of it, and that should be all that needs to be said. And that we are going to pay them.

"The same government that is asking all this has driven culture into the gutter and made it so difficult for bands to make any proper money that they have to sleep on settees and hitchhike to get from city to city. Basically, [they're saying] you shouldn't be paid very much because you enjoy it while you do it. I'm still spending quite a bit of time trying to make it happen so they can play for us on the Friday and then again on one of the later stages the day after."

Going back to Unconference – Danny explained they wouldn't now be doing the previously mooted minibus as they didn't want to take too much away from the festival on the day. But they would still extend the invitation of a visit to everyone there on the Friday. Anyone still there on the Sunday (the day after the festival) could come then. Danny also hoped they would have virtual tours online by then and "to be honest, after Friday and Unconference I wouldn't mind just having a jolly and a drink, because I love Twisterella".

As much as Danny would be able to let his hair down at the festival there would still be plenty to promote on the day. Readers might recall that the previous year, the Press On banner made its first appearance as the backdrop of the Westgarth 1 stage at the Westgarth Social Club, where it reappeared again this year. A combined FairSound/ Twisterella banner would similarly grace the stage for the Play Brew Co launch, and a FairSound: Powered by Press On one would be on show at the festival on the day.

Danny was also expecting an exclusive *Music Week* article to coincide with the launch (which did appear on 17 October[51]), so still plenty of positive publicity without oversaturating the festival itself. According to Danny, even at this stage, labels like Bella Union had already shown an interest in FairSound. "Crates[52] and Bandcamp do similar things they just haven't got a pressing plant. They've got the backend system and the website and all that, but the same problems as everyone else [with pressing times and product shortages]."

So, finally, after months of telling me about it, FairSound would be launched. It was then that the penny really dropped for me that FairSound wasn't anything to do with Rough Trade or Norman Records. I remembered a previous conversation where Danny had been fizzing about Bandcamp selling out to Epic Games, and I realised that all the talk about FairSound outliving Press On and revolutionising the industry wasn't just talk, but that they had genuinely laid

---

51   'Press On Vinyl Launches E-commerce Platform To Remove Financial Barriers For Artists And Labels', Andrew Paine, 17 October 2022, https://www.musicweek.com/labels/read/press-on-vinyl-launches-e-commerce-platform-to-remove-financial-barriers-for-artists-and-labels/086765. *Music Week* is a trade publication for the UK record industry distributed via a website and a monthly print magazine.

52   Crates is an electronic music browser "made by DJs for DJs". That's it. It is exactly that.

the foundations to usurp Bandcamp as the world's biggest supporter of independent music and unsigned artists.

"Hopefully we'll have a good understanding of music and try to bring new products to market like the sugar vinyl. Eventually we will also be able to bring costs down as the world starts to even itself out." Danny always had a canny way with a phrase that reminded me of a young Noel Gallagher, although it must be said, at this point we were only a few weeks away from the mini-budget in September 2022 – the one that collapsed the pound and nearly took the UK economy off the cliff with it.

I suggested to Danny that Press On as a company seemed to have already evened itself out since the so-called Mayhem back in May, so I was taken aback by his honest response. "We've had a nightmare in the galvanics, actually. Six weeks of torture. Out of nowhere we just had loads of pops and clicks on the records, and I mean like fireworks.

"That yellow vinyl I asked Laurence to do earlier, he's going to bring it back in a minute and that could be the answer. We think it was a little bit to do with the pressing, a little bit to do with the RO water[53], a little bit to do with the air quality, and a little bit to do with our chemicals being stored correctly. We are slowly working backwards to figure out exactly where the problems are occurring." Luckily, through relationships already built during the last year, they had been able to outsource their stampers for the previous three weeks, "So we are managing, but the test press Laurence will bring back in will hopefully say one way or the other whether what we have introduced today is gonna

---

53   Reverse Osmosis water, which is 99% pure and used to rinse the silvered lacquer.

work. I came in at half-four this morning cos I couldn't sleep, and [I] came in ready to do these tests." It was now just after 6pm.

"It's not like we are not producing and sending goods out of the door; we've found a way again. But it's definitely not going swimmingly... we don't actually think that is possible." Danny had recently been to Vinyl Presents in Hitchin to see their pressing operation, and had also visited the Vinyl Factory in London, as well as his Making Vinyl trip. "Every vinyl manufacturer has said it never just works, every day."

While Stamper Discs in Sheffield had helped Press On before, and although they have a very good relationship, they were at full capacity, so Vinyl Presents stepped in this time. While they may be a rival pressing plant, the UK market is so small it would be pointless for the plants to compete against each other, and for Press On every cloud is a silver-lined relationship to be built. "Building those relationships is vital, and the humility that has been reciprocated by Vinyl Presents is well received. They even congratulated us on getting this far. It felt a bit cap in hand to us, but it wasn't really like that."

I asked Danny more about the new 24/5 shift pattern, as this was something initially mentioned for March or April. He explained that from an operational point of view, the press was not far from him and Toddy not needing to be there. Peter (Haste, Engineer) and Kilvo, under the expert tutelage of Man, were now more than competent pressing engineers and line managers. But Danny was cautious of moving forward too quickly, which explains the slow progress to the new shifts, and the reluctance to move to a full 24/7 model.

Clearly speaking from experience: "You start running at full capacity and you get complacent and then you start overlooking things like maintenance, and that invariably comes back and bites you in the arse, and it's another massive lesson learned. I think things have been so hard that when they start going well the tendency is to have a jolly but, no, that's probably the time to double down on the other bits you need to do.

"I don't think we have to be here all the time, but I hope everybody wants us to be here. We are good to bounce ideas off and also to share in their success when things go well. We've got an office upstairs we haven't moved into yet." In fact, this was another thing first mentioned way back in October. The room had always been there for that purpose, but still needed properly boarding out and plastering. "I hope we move in there before Christmas, because we do get distracted down here but at the same time... it's hard to find that balance. However, if you go up there now it is full of Avalanche Party's gear. They've got an album to finish off so it would be nice to think they might finish it here.

"Before COVID, when we had the studio at Sticky Fingers in Middlesbrough, we could go 24/7. We thought we'd made it, being able to go out on the session and then go back to the studio. I just feel for [Avalanche Party] and how hollow that must have felt when [their last] place flooded and they couldn't stay anymore. Not only that, it is potentially a lot of expensive gear being damaged. I'm glad we could help. Toddy just phoned me up, cos I was in London, and said he'd made an executive decision to move Avalanche Party into our office.

"Be a good person. If you can do something good, just do it. [Their stuff] stinks, but we'll forgive them for that..."

I asked about the North American consultant's ongoing role in all this, as he seemed to play a vital part in all major decisions over the last 12 months, and his influence on the early Press On Vinyl set-up can't be downplayed. I might lightheartedly think of him as that background Simpsons character, but on-call since day one, like many of the company's inner-circle, he was pivotal in introducing the full end-to-end process the plant has at its disposal. Without the galvanics lab, for sure, Press On Vinyl would not have been able to come through on their 16-week lead time promise. Danny hoped he would be full-time for Press On at some point in 2023, leading FairSound globally, in charge of finding new plants as the brand grows, and sourcing raw product and pressing parts at competitive prices.

And the relationship with the unnamed big record label? "I had dinner with them last week, actually. They took me out for a lovely vegetarian lunch, and they've put some more work our way. They put us in touch with [other labels], too. They are very accommodating, but I just think they think 'What the fuck?!'. They are not disparaging in any way; they are helpful." If this *does* come across as a little disparaging, then maybe it is. There is a smug arrogance about this label's business approach, and I can't help feeling they might just be biding their time waiting for Press On to slip up. But only time will tell.

As if scripted, in came Clancy with another test press, and as he placed it on the deck Danny was already on his feet, spinning the volume up and looking for the sweet spot in the room (spoiler: he knew where it was). They had narrowed the problem down to the air quality and that was what this particular fix was aimed at eradicating. "When the silver is put on the lacquer for silvering, it needs air to push the silver on. We use nitrogen-free hydrogen, which is the cleanest air you can get. We have to buy that, but also the nitrogen-free air allows the particles of the silver and the sugar to moleculise [sic], so it's two-fold really. We've been here before, where you get kicked in the teeth. So, this is the moment of truth where we find out if what we introduced today has worked."

Suddenly, from the speakers, there came a singular looping bass groove, and a couple of seconds later a driving 70s orchestral hook immediately took me back to the funk and soul clubs of my youth, and the Nuggets tapes my friends and I shared at university. But for Danny this was something else entirely. Validation. As the groove dropped out for a gospel chorus so slick it kept my toe tapping until it came back in, Danny was pure buzzing.

"That's eight weeks in the making that test press. It's not definitely right, but it sounds class…" And do you know what? It really did. As I left for the day through the front door into the carpark, Danny exited stage left, back out onto the factory floor. All I could hear was a quietening "Motherfuckerrrs!" as the soft-close door slowly swung shut behind him.

Day 360
4 October 2022

With a few days to go before Twisterella festival, I arrived at Press On Vinyl on an unseasonably cold and miserable Tuesday morning. I found the office bristling with an enthusiasm I hadn't seen since the original Komparrison test presses came off the machines in January, or Yussef's official opening of the first two pressing machines in February. The usually serene office area was full of the characters I had heard about, if not spoken to. Man was now resident in the UK, and Franco was flying back in later that day. Elsewhere in the office some sharp suits and expensive leather shoes also gave away the importance of the next few days for Press On Vinyl.

Danny was deep in conversation with Blood Records representatives and the guys from Evolution Music. Later that day the Michael Stipe record, the first bioplastic record in the world to be commercially produced and sold, was due to be pressed. This accounted for the low-level anxiety that seemed to infiltrate the general bonhomie. For context, Blood Records basically have something of a monopoly over picture discs and other designer vinyl, so a tie-in with Press On would be something of a big deal, while the bioplastics development would certainly revolutionise vinyl-making in the future, whether that be one, two or five years down the line.

Colin was busy flitting around between various meetings and also overseeing the Michael Stipe press, which was ready to go any minute and an indicator of how important the official FairSound launch on the Friday would be.

Everyone was well reminded that Friday was a work event and that they should enjoy themselves but not *too* much. The only dampener was that Love'n'Joy would be unable to play the event or Twisterella festival the following day, due to the ongoing visa problems that had blighted their efforts to visit the UK all year. However, Girl From Winter Jargon had been more than willing, and capable, to step in and perform at the last minute. Regarding Love'n'Joy, Danny would tell me (although it wasn't his fault at all) that the whole episode was the most embarrassing of his life. Another example, if one was needed, of how personally he takes everything.

Later in the day, even the North American consultant arrived straight from Newcastle Airport after a few seconds of panic back at HQ that a driver had not been sent to collect him. Luckily, Kilvo was on the case.

Up in Alex's mastering suite, the room was fully tuned. They were still waiting for the front wall baffle boards to be installed, but it looked much like any other mastering suite, albeit with a few more gadgets and instruments what with having the live room immediately downstairs. Alex explained that also having the plant just downstairs wouldn't have any impact on how he works and was keen to point out a few things that still needed doing but they were mostly cosmetic. The ceiling boards, or clouds as he called them, still needed tweaking; position was key. He was also still properly linking the rooms together technically. Another visitor to the plant around this time told me he had shown a couple of photos of the mastering suite to some techie friends of his who had "lost their shit" at how high-end it was already looking.

Crucially, immediately adjacent to the mastering suite on the mezzanine floor, the lathe was now set up in the corner of the small cutting room that had previously always been behind a padlocked door. A similar deadness in the sound when the door shut behind me added a certain (hushed) reverence to the oddly retro-futuristic scene that stood to play a pivotal role in Press On phase two.

With everything else going on around him, Toddy was hard at work putting some final touches to the FairSound beta site, which already looked slick and easy to use. He gleefully told me they had someone working on an animation that would see the yellow dot above the 'i' in FairSound transformed into stickmen, records and the wheels of a delivery van (something Danny would elaborate on a bit later).

When I spoke to Colin in June, I had asked him the same question I asked Danny back in January, about where, realistically, he saw the business being in five years' time. He was clearly focused on the importance of greener business practices. However, even at this stage of the bioplastic development a rival product, which was attempting to reverse-engineer the existing process by removing the oil from the vinyl mix to reduce the carbon footprint of the product, was already vying for a share of the market, and with better sound quality to date than the bioplastic version.

Colin told me, with the bioplastic compound the main development at the time: "My core business is promoting and I've just got permission to put on a concert I've been trying to do for years in the centre of Leeds which will be completely carbon neutral, and that includes generators, solar panels, local produce, dealing with all the waste locally, encouraging people not to come in cars, or at least providing facilities for electric cars and bikes and so on. For Press On to go down the bio-compound route totally makes sense as an extension of that."

While it may have been good fortune that the pressing machines at Press On seem to cope with the new compound better than other machines elsewhere, it still felt like a natural progression for the company. "We are not going to take our eye off the ball, and this doesn't affect what we are doing as a company as far as the pressing plant goes because it just means, do we use, in the future, PVC or do we use a bio-compound? At the moment it's not easy to switch between the two, and it's all trial and error but we are trying to get there and this new compound that has just arrived today..." tweaked a little now, with talc in it to try and remove the need for the mould release that was causing the unusual sheen on the vinyl and the strange breezy sound on playback.

When I returned to the office, the bioplastic release that Press On had been test pressing just a few weeks before was about to go to press, with all the bigwigs watching.

But unfortunately the new talc-infused compound left a white mark on the stamper. Even after a good hour of TLC from Chad (Matthew Howard, Team Leader Pressing Operator), the marking was stubborn enough that the attempt was eventually aborted. A last-minute switch to the original bio-compound was also not possible, meaning the big event would have to be postponed until the next day so that a new stamper could be grown overnight. The atmosphere in the office was a little strained, but the mantra was very much 'this is how it is now, this is normal' and they were right. No business is ever plain sailing.

Colin: "We do a festival called Live At Leeds, and Dance to the Radio [one of Colin's business imprints] are taking over Hyde Park Book Club, and we are doing a compilation bio-compound album for the day." I remembered chewing the fat once with Danny about how cool compilation albums are. "We are getting there, but it's a lot of work for such a small improvement in product. But this new compound should press better. Going forward with that and then actually producing the compound in Teesside as well will be amazing. It will be great for [the area] and great for us as a business. ... I can imagine a lot of companies that have 20, 40 or 100 machines knocking out your Adeles and re-runs of Fleetwood Mac don't want those machines to stop and don't want us to change the status quo, but if we can come up with a compound at the same price...

"We look at it commercially, but we are not as obviously completely commercial because we are ideas people, and we are doing it for the greater good, for bands, for labels. But if you are watching those pennies come in as a commercial company, you are not going to want to make a change like that in case it upsets your revenues. It's easier for us to do it because we can keep our vinyl ticking over while we are experimenting a bit."

It was certainly easy to get carried away by the ethical opportunities provided by such a development but, as ever,

Colin was cautious about just how revolutionary a change it might herald: "I don't think it's going to completely get rid of vinyl. If you look back to the 70s and 80s, there were loads of crap Top of the Pops albums and those are the ones that are ending up in landfill or being turned into flowerpots. It seems to be people that are passionate about the music that are making vinyl collectible for the artists they follow, so when they get that album it is more likely to be passed on or sold on because it has value. So, you will always have that, but the bio-compound will overtake it most probably. [It will eventually become cheaper to manufacture], but that is going to take time."

With the sustainability seal having been broken for the event in Leeds, Colin was keen to start using the same advances in green delivery for future events. A change in the law also meant events were no longer allowed to use red diesel meaning, notwithstanding increased energy prices anyway, things were getting a lot more expensive.

"Our diesel bill went from £14,000 to £38,000 just for one event. The bad thing about that is it cost us loads of money, but the good thing is it has made everybody think about using reusable energy or finding other ways of doing things. The long-term goal for this plant is to be 100% carbon neutral. It was built before we got here, we didn't commission it, so we walked into something we are reusing, and then if the energy comes from hydrogen, solar panels or... the river is right there. And the more we go down this road with the bio compound and using food for the energy and for the product, you are already in the mix."

With things moving this fast it was no wonder Colin and Danny's visions may have differed slightly, but one thing that was clear was that in a part of the music industry that had not moved forward for decades, something or someone was causing other areas to focus on more environmentally friendly ways of doing things.

There is this romantic imagining of the music industry as an ecosystem where many symbiotic relationships hold everything together, and while this might have been true in Danny's vision of the Detroit heyday, in actual fact it can be the wildest of the wests at times. But Danny and Colin's unswerving belief in sustainability and inclusivity might well go on to restore that, or at least some faith in that – or, at the very least, some faith in that for independent artists.

A quick stop for pizza and things could only get better – until an Andrew Cushin lacquer, delivered that morning ahead of his imminent UK tour, was scratched, meaning he wouldn't have any vinyl to sell on the opening night. Another reason for doing the cutting in-house. Gareth had the unenviable job of ringing Jai Stanley (who is also Pete Doherty's manager), at the pair's Strap Originals label, to tell him. These things, as they were already well on the way to realising, are sent to test them.

With everything else going on in the office, I managed to pin Danny down for ten minutes in between slices of pizza. He was as keen as Toddy to show me around the FairSound website. "We've been trying to get a good cross-section of genres and artists for the beta test. I'm really proud of it, and we've spent a lot of time on it. That's what I've been working on mostly. Really informative, really easy to use, plain, simple. We are going to do a little animation with the orange dot on the 'i' of FairSound which will be our logo at every stage, even making [it] the wheels on the van as he drives off to deliver the records." I immediately noticed a little freehand underline, which could become equally distinctive in an Amazon sort of way, such that it was obvious straight away that this was a slick and well-designed website.

Danny had also spent quite a bit of time recently in London speaking to labels like Communion, Acid Jazz, Rough Trade and Bella Union. "I still go in with a bit of imposter syndrome, but we are so well received, and they really want to work with us, so it has not been a sales effort at all, more of a getting-to-know-you effort. We are getting ready for the next two pressing machines which got packed up last week and will be here next month." November, but this would be revised to December. "We've got more cells coming in January for the galvanics. We are building a recycling facility on-site, and just about finishing off the mastering suite and recording studio."

There was some chatter about Elton John coming to the plant, and the Beckstein grand piano that had previously been housed at Bad Neighbour Records (and used by Komparrison back in March for their EP launch) had already taken pride of place in the live room. Elton had apparently shown an interest in the plant pressing a bioplastic record for him. "That will be February [2023] probably. If Michael Stipe and Elton John can get it off the ground, then it needs to be mass produced so we can get it cheaper. We want to use it on FairSound so it will be accessible for independents as well, because they are younger and it's them that are leading the charge. It's great Michael Stipe and Elton John are raising the profile, but we need these other people to run with it."

Since the last time I visited there had been no further issues with the galvanics. However, the Love'n'Joy situation was still unresolved, and everyone felt partly responsible for that which, of course, they weren't. Later the same month I happened to bump into Danny and he was pleased to tell me the band had now secured their visa and would finally be in the UK in November. Now there was just the small matter of a UK tour to be arranged.

Day 365
8 October 2022

As the autumn sun rose over the Press On Vinyl plant for another day, Danny may have had a couple more wrinkles and Tommy's beard was much longer and a little greyer, but the same infectious ebullience and enthusiasm persisted as had been there since day one.

To date, the plant had pressed around 250,000 records, with a target of 1.5 million in 2023 once the next two pressing machines arrived. Press On Vinyl had run around 300 different jobs, including 150 for fully independent artists. Danny estimated they had about ten labels putting in repeat orders, and then a further 20 regular requests including Ninja, Alcopop, Blitz Cat, Opus Kink's Nice One label, Bella Union and Communion, all of which had orders scheduled on the office white board as we spoke.

Press On were also working with brokers such as Curved, VDC and Cram who (while 'broker' was seen as a dirty word at the start of the Press On Vinyl story) Danny embraced as a crucial part of the bigger picture. The added bonus was that the brokers arranged their own artwork, so it was much quicker for Press On to ship the vinyl out of the factory door without any of the potential hold-ups that had caused some major cash flow problems earlier in the year. There was even talk of giving over some capacity just for the brokers – but no more than 40,000 records per month. However, Danny was keen to stress that there would never be a situation where a small order would be held up because of these types of arrangements, and that as FairSound continued to grow it would ensure that.

At present, this was mostly UK sales, but already around 5% of the records pressed at the plant were being shipped abroad – although partners such as Ninja Tunes and Blood Records were taking delivery and then distributing to their buyers themselves, so that figure may have been significantly higher.

In the next couple of months Press On Vinyl would finally take receipt of the two new pressing machines, and with them would come the beginnings of phase two of the Press On Vinyl story.

Twenty-seven staff on the books and a handful of regular freelancers already on board meant the company was well on the way to the initial target of 38 staff to secure funding from FW Capital through their grant system. This grant equates to roughly £10,000 per job created, and the Press On's projection was to reach that threshold by January 2023, once the two additional pressing machines were up and running. "We'll probably reach that target within a year of being operational, and that target for the grants that we pledged to Tees Valley Combined Authority was initially for four years," Danny told me. "We'll probably have all the staff but still be owed about one third of the money, which shows you how quickly we have expanded."

Day 365 – 8 October – was also the day that Press On Vinyl would finally officially launch FairSound into the world.

Since day one, FairSound had always been the cherry on the Press On Vinyl cake. Danny and Tommy had initially enthused about how the flagship platform would outlive and outperform Press On. Although a couple of rethinks resulted in them taking a step back and focusing on its initial purpose as a platform for artists to crowdfund and distribute their music and merch, free from bullshit.

The big selling point at this stage, and a mantra I heard Danny repeat a number of times to various people, was that FairSound was a distribution platform that removed the delays caused in vinyl production by having its own pressing plant attached. It guaranteed a 16-week lead time; distributed and sold these records without taking a commission (the big gazump on Bandcamp); and offered a no-obligation 30-day crowdfunder service to make all this happen.

For sure, plans at one point were much bigger than that, including a social media sub-platform. That kind of thing might still happen in the future, but for now its current form was enough, and a final example of Danny and Toddy's continued commitment to doing the right thing for Press On, for the music industry, and for everyone.

With Man now in the UK permanently; Franco still committed to making Press On the best pressing plant in the world; North American consultant consulting; Alex loving his new mezzanine deck; and Colin also in it for the long haul, the stage was set, almost literally... The night before the FairSound socials went live, at an event which had originally been billed as a Twisterella opening party, Play Brew Co (a venue a stone's throw from the plant, in Middlesbrough's Newport area), formally launched the FairSound project.

I tagged along with Danny to Twisterella's flagship Unconference on the morning before the main event, to listen to him and Toddy talk enthusiastically about all things Press On Vinyl one last time. This was a chance for all in attendance to hear about FairSound for the first time, and find out what Press On could do for them – because that is what this story had always been about: what can Press On Vinyl do for us, do for Teesside, and do for the music industry?

The talk was attended by a mixture of young artists attending the festival (exactly who the initial rollout of FairSound was really aimed at) and locally based industry veterans keen to learn more about the platform. For Danny and Toddy, it was obvious they were keen to see the reaction from those gathered, while their brains continued to work at double speed to process all the ideas bouncing around the informal roundtable format. I thought it would be interesting to follow the Press On Vinyl socials over the coming months to see if any of the artists in attendance, or the ideas floated, were followed up.

On the morning of the festival, FairSound's socials suddenly appeared, to little fanfare. It would not be until ten days later, on 18 October, that these social channels actually launched, at 12pm, with a flurry of activity on Facebook, Twitter and Instagram. Though perhaps a little underwhelming given that the Twisterella background noise was practically non-existent on the day of the launch.

In the afternoon, the festival itself allowed Danny and Toddy to relax a bit more. It was nice to see them and a number of their staff sticking together as a group even late into the day. Franco was there with his backpack, the intrepid pro; Man with a perma-grin, while Kilvo and Papa Goose introduced them to the sights and sounds of Twisterella, including Jodie Nicholson – now with a full band behind her, and promoted to the main Teesside University stage. It was particularly nice to see the genuine friendship that had formed between Kilvo and Man: the Morrison's van guy and the Japanese pressing impresario.

It was difficult at this stage to envisage how FairSound could ever increase its market share beyond Press On's limited capacity, and I started to see that even the notion that FairSound demand might outstrip Press On quite quickly could be a little further down the line in reality – never mind challenging Bandcamp for market dominance. Even Colin Oliver's anticipated long-term vinyl production aim of 1.5 to 2 million units per annum would only account for some 20 to 25% of total vinyl production in the UK. While this would be as significant an impact on the industry as Colin had always talked about, it would never be enough on its own to herald a complete changing of the old guard.

Without much in the way of pre-advertising, initial engagement with the FairSound beta website and specifically sales (which are visible on the site to anyone) were slow. It remained to be seen if FairSound would be a game changer other than to those in the North East and others lucky enough to be using Press On Vinyl for pressing purposes. At the end of day two, a cursory look at the website (even a Google search still showed the site under construction and nowhere near the top of the search) showed the first legacy artist reissue, Dartz! debut *This Is My Ship*, already 38 pre-orders towards their target of 100. However, Butterfly Effect's The Shining Levels album had only one pre-sale, while Love'n'Joy had three.

Everything usually moved fast where Press On Vinyl were concerned, but even by their own breathless standards, the vinyl market was really starting to jockey for position. A flurry of Press On news activity coincided with the FairSound social media launch, including the *Music Week* article Danny had mentioned, and another on *Gigwise*[54]. But it was an article on *Bdaily*[55], an online publisher of UK regional business news, that caught the eye of some industry experts.

The site ran the usual broadly positive narrative about Press On, but on the same day the same site was pushing a similar article about another so-called revolutionary vinyl venture for on-demand vinyl where, conceivably, any title ever recorded could be made available on vinyl through a mysterious mix of patent-pending technology and science. Tellingly there was no firm detail on this London-based start-up, and it wasn't clear whether this was a pressing plant or whether that plant might include a galvanics lab and/or recording and mastering facilities. But it was another small victory in the Press On story, as other start-ups began unapologetically taking Danny and Toddy's enthusiasm for

---

54 'Press On Vinyl Are Making Records More Accessible', 17 October 2022, https://gigwise.com/news/3427334/press-on-vinyl-are-making-records-more-accessible.

55 'Teesside Record Plant Press On Vinyl Launch Platform To Help Artists And Labels', Mark Adair, 18 October 2022, https://bdaily.co.uk/articles/2022/10/18/teesside-record-plant-press-on-vinyl-launch-platform-to-help-artists-and-labels.

doing things differently and seeing where they themselves might also be able to take things. A revolution brewing? Perhaps. Just be careful where you leave that Cuban flag.

Elsewhere on Press On's socials it was business as usual, with factory staff showing off various coloured vinyls, Andy (Harker, Packing and Logistics Coordinator) with a lovely pair of blues. Danny and Tommy did a little video interview in front of the microphones with Breakout Media, a local digital marketing company, where Tommy looked a little bemused while Danny went through his, by now well-honed, FairSound pitch, as well as the serious business of promoting FairSound, which was now taking up more than half of Press On's Facebook feed.

Danny told me the mastering suite was all but complete and they were just waiting for someone to come and commission the lathe. This was the final piece in the Phase One jigsaw – but then he hit me with a complete curveball.

"So, we tested another bio-compound for INEOS[56] the other day. They are doing it differently to Evolution Music, as they are working back from PVC, so the first [stage] of it is to remove all the fossil fuel oil out of it and replace it with a natural ethanol and you wanna hear it, it's incredible. The first phase is a 75% reduction in the carbon footprint already. It's not completely recyclable *yet*, but it will be, because the compound to make the black pigment in the second phase will use old car tyres instead of carbon, so it's actually carbon positive."

---

56 INEOS is a global chemical company with an office in nearby Newton Aycliffe which saw Hydro Polymers become part of the INEOS family in 2008. INEOS is also widely known as a sponsor of a team in the Tour de France, in line with its consumer brands and sports interests.

Danny then played me a Dance to the Radio record made with the new compound. It was indeed impressive, with barely any audible surface noise as it blasted through the office. He explained how INEOS had still been putting the final touches to the compound at 2am the night before, and that they had pressed the record while they were on-site at 10am the next morning.

Danny told me Press On had managed to press 500 of the Evolution Music Michael Stipe records, but they had noticeable surface noise compared to PVC records. Press On were worried that that would need highlighting to buyers, so that people understood the bioplastic was still in development, and so they weren't put off vinyl by a product that was still being finetuned. It was telling that his main concern was the broader vinyl industry and not the fact the flagship product had been produced at his own plant.

Certainly, there is no reason the two products can't eventually co-exist if they are similar quality (although some readers might remember the intricacies of the VHS/Betamax head-to-head).

"We are in a great position, where people want to work with us, and [we're] at the level of INEOS wanting to develop something with us here in Middlesbrough. which is great for us and them and the industry, so…"

Listening to Danny talk enthusiastically about what phase two of Press On Vinyl might bring, I couldn't imagine his passion for the project ever diminishing. But for him (and Toddy) it had clearly been a steep learning curve and not one that would completely level off any time soon, if ever. I recalled the night before Twisterella, at the FairSound launch at Play Brew Co, where it had been interesting to note the change in demeanour and general behaviour since the last launch party at Sticky's in Stockton way back in January.

In January, there had been a party atmosphere: drinks were flowing and backs were being slapped – but it was really little more than a bunch of likeminded Teessiders celebrating their friends setting up something good. The mood at Play Brew Co, as a yardstick for how the business now conducted itself generally, was much more studied. Drinks were taken, but in moderation. The faces in attendance were internationally renowned.

Many of the people in attendance had come to Teesside for Twisterella the next day. They were at the launch to see what all the chatter was about, and to network, not celebrate. The night featured Durham's extraordinary loop-pedal experimenter Girl From Winter Jargon – her booking another reminder, if one was needed, of Press On's continued commitment to the local scene and artist development, along with the company's ongoing obligation to customer service. And that's when it suddenly dawned on me what this was all ever really about:

Two best mates hanging out, making each other laugh and putting on gigs for their friends. Having then found nobody was able to help with something else they wanted to do, their natural instinct was to do it themselves. They just wanted to make a record.

Epilogue
Christmas Eve 2022

Christmas Eve 2022 was a Saturday those fortunate enough to work a Monday-to-Friday week will remember as a bonus day off before the main event, as if Christmas had never fallen on a Sunday before. For everyone at Press On Vinyl it was also the start of a well-earned ten-day break. Since the FairSound launch at Twisterella in October plenty had been going on…

A week after Twisterella, in mid-October, the Dartz! re-release was nearly up to its pre-order target on FairSound. For a legacy band this was impressive, although an amount of local prestige would have always seen it over the line. Two others on the beta launch were already ticking along nicely, but others were lagging, with Danny a little irked that the artists were not promoting FairSound more themselves. After all, it was their fans that would be buying the records.

FairSound had never been designed as a new marketplace, but more somewhere to facilitate sales cheaply and all in one place. Harry from Hanglands had worked extensively on the website and he was already planning a competition-style advertising campaign in magazines including *DIY* and *Kerrang!* as well as a jazz and dance magazine where one artist would get a free vinyl run as a prize. This would allow Press On to advertise FairSound more widely – it was always intended for all genres.

As ever, Danny had a slight twist he wanted to introduce to the genre mix, partly to outline the positive language of the new profit sheets they were sending out with order enquiries: "I'd really like to get a school choir or something like that on there. If an artist sells 1,000 records, they can make £15k. We like to stay away from that [kind of thing], but [profit] is why people are doing it, to monetise the product. Not so much with a run of 100, but for 200 and above there is a decent amount of profit."

His thinking was that a school choir would have a lot of parents as potential customers, but equally important to him was the sense of community he was keen to instil in the FairSound delivery by involving schools and/or choirs. It was his way of providing for the community. Danny then told me another one of his unbelievable, but totally true, stories about how as kids he and Middlesbrough-born pastor Rikki Doolan once snuck into a church on Clive Road in Middlesbrough because they'd heard some music. Once inside, Danny claimed he and Rikki saw a preacher healing a woman. The pair made an equally quick escape with Danny, in particular, being slightly traumatised by what he had seen, while for Rikki it may have been more of an epiphany.

In the couple of months since the FairSound launch there had been lots of visits to the plant from record labels including Acid Jazz, Communion and Earache, while the Opus Kink connection was increasingly cemented, with them penned in as almost a house band. Danny told me the plan was still for the first live-to-lathe to take place soon. "They are coming up for about 20 days to help us learn the room. They all have solo gigs as well, so they won't all be here all the time. We'll also maybe make a bit of a documentary of them all converging here and being creative."

And Danny also had one final curveball for me: "Toddy's gone mad!"

It turned out Toddy had been keeping busy designing a new magnetic induction mould, similar to the electric hobs some of us have in our kitchens, which was going to be powered by electricity from the solar panels Press On planned to have installed on the roof. The new mould would be retrofitted to the existing pressing machines. His idea would mean they could eventually remove the steam and gas works to be fully carbon neutral. Danny told me, "He's pulling loads of people together from the likes of The Welding Institute for grants, EFD[57] who do similar things with sustainable induction heating equipment but not record pressing, and an engineer we already know to actually make the mould."

Love'n'Joy were scheduled to come over in November but then put back again until January 2023, but Danny told

---

57   EFD Induction is a leading international green-tech company that supplies cost-effective, safe and energy-efficient induction heating solutions with offices all over the world. Toddy was not doing things by halves.

me their record would be getting pressed regardless of Press On Point being reached, and that there would be a big social media push around their UK dates when they did happen. He was clearly still smarting from the earlier visa fiasco and keen to make their first visit to the UK as successful and enjoyable as possible. (The group reached Press On Point on 18 November, ensuring the record would be pressed and distributed to fans directly from Middlesbrough.)

With the lathe calibrated and ready to *cut* the first record in Middlesbrough ten months after the first record was *pressed*, the big reveal on Press On socials took place on 14 December. The first commercial cut, touchingly the Dartz! record (complete with UTB[58] scratched into the run-out groove Porky's[59] style), took place two days later, on 16 December.

It is difficult to overstate the importance of the lathe announcement. Although the lathe was not a secret (plenty of people had already had sight of it in situ, or at least the locked door it had been stored behind these last few weeks) even those following the Press On social feeds closely might

---

58   Up The Boro.
59   George Peckham was a mastering engineer at Apple Studios in London (Apple as in The Beatles' Apple Corp venture in the late 1960s and not the Californian tech company of some renown) who started adding humorous notes to the run-out grooves of albums he had mastered as the wax lacquer was so easy to inscribe. The messages were often signed 'Porky', 'A Porky Prime Cut' or various other iterations of the theme.

have been unaware a lathe had already been purchased, even if it was the obvious missing piece of the jigsaw. Not only that, but the Neumann VMS80 at the Press On plant was one of the best lathes still available and the team were only then able to announce that they would be moving forward with master cutting with guidance and support from Pete Norman and Lewis Hopkins of Stardelta Audio Mastering, alongside Alex Balzama. This would be Pete and Lewis' first official recognition in the Press On Vinyl story so far.

The same day Press On Vinyl also announced a FairSound/*DIY Magazine* partnership, with some gigs scheduled for January 2023 at London's Old Blue Last venue. Things started coming thick and fast again, an example of how far things had come since the proposed live link-up with Sticky Fingers in Middlesbrough first mooted back in December 2021.

On 23 December the Press On team, including yours truly, had decamped again to the other Sticky's in Stockton for Press On's Christmas party. When I arrived, Toddy was absent altogether with a stomach bug, and I was surprised to find Danny somewhat out of sorts. It was clear something else was going on in the background. It was also an unexpectedly low-key, poorly turned-out affair, if typically boozy. Danny told me he was still disappointed he hadn't managed to meet First Aid Kit[60] at their Leeds show a couple of weeks before. He had hoped to ask the Swedish duo about a little Middlesbrough link I had mentioned to him a while back,

---

60   First Aid Kit are a Swedish country-folk duo consisting of siblings Johanna and Klara Söderberg. Their grandfather was Pastor Lennart Lundström, who led the congregation at the Swedish Church in Middlesbrough in the 1970s.

which was classic Danny, and I took this little anecdote of his to be a symptom rather than the cause of his mental malaise. Tommy was three-sheets-to-the-wind but bouncing around talking to anybody that would listen, and only Kerry really seemed to be her usual self. Elsewhere in the cavernous bar pool balls were sunk, darts thrown, and a general bonhomie was present if not entirely prevalent, although Jordan from Avalanche Party was quietly holding court at the bar, as Jordan likes to do.

Danny also admitted to me, for the first time, that Press On Vinyl would soon start making a lot of money and that he was uncomfortable with that, already wanting to find a way of giving it all back to the town.

It was an admirable stance, but one he would do well to consider carefully. Firstly, because a small cabal of businessmen seemingly monopolised much of the town's investments, which was not exactly in keeping with the Press On Vinyl ethos I have written so much about and so, presumably, was not something Danny would likely want to be seen as being in cahoots with. And secondly, because of what Danny had already given back to the town through the priceless positive media Press On Vinyl had attracted after years of Middlesbrough being a go-to for poverty clickbait; the jobs he and the team had already helped create; and the money Press On were already generating for the area (not just the profit margin for the company itself).

However, when I told him this it seemed to do little to lift him from this surprising conflict, even when I suggested that, after years of grafting various jobs for other people, maybe it was just his time.

The next day I returned to the Press On plant for one final visit. It seemed fitting, a year to the day after the first two pressing machines had arrived. It was partly for a catch up, but mainly as a sort of debrief – to purge my extruder, as it were. Things had moved so fast for Press On Vinyl over the past 12 months I was concerned that a lot more would happen before this book was published so, with my print deadline approaching, there was just time to add these final few paragraphs about the plant's progress in the three months since my last visit as part of Twisterella festival in October.

The mezzanine boardroom where I had talked to Emma and Kerry about the mental health effects of managing such an operation was now fitted out with some shelving, another high-end turntable system, Avalanche Party's drum kit, and a selection of furniture recently salvaged from the BaseCamp fire sale after their flood and subsequent closure in late 2022.

Sitting there, the room had an unusual anti-space feel to it. Dark, enclosed and oddly subdued compared to the sprawling factory floor and colourful main office downstairs. Perhaps somewhere Danny and Toddy would do well to take advantage of, to take themselves away from the pressures of the day. The corner window, where the drum kit was, looked out over the warehouse, while the Newport Bridge and River Tees view from the opposite corner was a post-industrial diorama.

Danny was still not his usual self, but would later admit, when I asked about the general stress levels, that he had been suffering crippling anxiety at the prospect of closing the plant for ten days over the holiday period.

The two new pressing machines were scheduled to arrive on 4 January 2023 (these would be blue) but there were still no plans for the factory to move to being open 24/7. Danny was keen to maintain a work/life balance for his staff while also wanting to be free to use the live room as much as possible on weekends. The five-day week also allowed for any emergency overtime if any further problems arose in the factory.

The live room looked far from finished when Danny showed me it again, but he assured me it would be ready for use by mid-January, and Opus Kink were still on standby to road-test it. There would also be an Opus Kink show at Middlesbrough's Westgarth Social Club in late January featuring Avalanche Party, Jodie Nicholson and, at long last, Love'n'Joy. The first live-to-lathe from Opus Kink was pencilled in for March, with Pete Norman.

FairSound was still at beta stage but was expected to go fully live by April at the latest.

On the bio-plastics front things remained a little uncertain. As of December 2022 Press On were still working with both INEOS and Evolution Music on their respective projects, but Danny explained he and Toddy were urging caution, as the sound quality wasn't yet up to Press On's exacting standards.

What I was personally most excited to hear about, though, was news that Toddy's induction mould project was still moving along nicely. It already felt like a symbol of Press On Vinyl phase two's increasingly green push, which still very much included the solar panels on the roof and the on-site recycling facility.

I had asked Danny back in February 2022 where he saw the company in October the same year and his very to-the-point answer was "four [pressing] machines, 24/7". Now, in late December, he wasn't far wrong: the 24/5 model was fully justified, and testament to the hard work, planning and conviction that had seen so much achieved in the 15 months I had been visiting the site.

As a neat little addendum to this whole story, on 27 December 2022 it was announced that UK vinyl sales in 2022 had outstripped CD sales for the first time since the 1980s, with the *Guardian*[61] describing it as a watershed moment for the vinyl revival. While that remains to be seen, it certainly set a new watermark for Press On's next year in business.

I remembered back to my very first visit to the Press On plant, nervously pitching the idea for this book to Danny, Tommy and Kerry in the half-finished galvanics lab. I didn't know what a galvanics lab was, then. I didn't know anything about making a record or the complex machinery and processes required to do it, and neither did they. Not

---

61 'Taylor Swift Propels UK Vinyl Sales Past CDs For First Time In 35 Years', Mark Sweney, 27 December 2022, https://www.theguardian.com/music/2022/dec/27/taylor-swift-propels-uk-vinyl-sales-past-cds-for-first-time-in-35-years.
The Guardian would also then run a further Spotlight feature on the company on New Year's Day: 'Turning Tables: The UK's New Vinyl Manufacturer Riding The Music Revival', Jessica Murray, 1 January 2023, https://www.theguardian.com/music/2023/jan/01/uk-vinyl-manufacturer-press-on-middlesbrough.

really. Now the same people, and others I met along the way, had become people I admire and respect for all that they are doing for the local area, the jobs they have created, and the relationships they are building with all they meet – and also their vison to make the music industry a fairer place for all.

It was easy, now, to see why everyone that worked there shared Franco's view that Press On Vinyl could indeed be the greatest pressing plant in the world.

GLOSSARY

extruder
Part of the pressing machine. Heated PVC pellets are fed from the hopper and propelled through the extruder into a cavity in the shape of a puck.

galvanics
Work relating to a direct current of electricity, in this case the process of electroforming the nickel stampers using the lacquer. The galvanics lab is a separate sealed room in the factory.

hopper
On the pressing machine the PVC pellets are loaded into the hopper, heated and then fed into the extruder.

lacquer
Wax disc used to produce a playable master record to go to the galvanics lab for silvering and electroplating.

lathe
The machine that cuts the groove into the lacquer.

live-to-lathe
Cutting the lacquer live in real time, using audio direct from a recording studio.

PVC pellets
Small loose plastic pellets in various colours. These are the raw material of a record.

silvering machine
Sprays the lacquer with a silvering solution in preparation for electroplating.

splatter disc
Unique splatter-patterned records made using a mix of different-coloured PVC pellets.

stamper
Made from nickel, this is a reverse image of the record itself. It is used to press the vinyl records that are ultimately played by music-lovers.

vinyl puck
Ice hockey puck-sized piece of soft, warmed PVC, made from PVC pellets. It is pressed into a record.

Acknowledgements

Stephen Gill at Butterfly Effect; Françoise Harvey; Danny, Toddy, Kerry and Tommy at Press On Vinyl; Tees Music Alliance; Sophie at Inpress Ltd; Scott Lewis at Clue Records; Henry Carden; Neil Spithray; Vivienne Hardman; Emma Dolby; Phil Saunders; Martha Lane; Dominic Dunn; Rob Irish; Graeme Wilkinson.